GOD'S UNCONDITIONAL LOVE

For
Jeneé
In Appreciation
For your
Dedicated Work
With Youth

Sheila & Naven

GOD'S UNCONDITIONAL LOVE

Healing Our Shame

WILKIE AU AND
NOREEN CANNON AU

Paulist Press
New York / Mahwah, NJ

Cover image by Zetta/Shutterstock.com
Cover and book design by Lynn Else

Library of Congress Cataloging-in-Publication Data

Au, Wilkie, 1944–
   God's unconditional love : healing our shame / Wilkie Au and Noreen Cannon Au.
      pages cm
   Includes bibliographical references.
   ISBN 978-0-8091-4961-2 (pbk. : alk. paper) — ISBN 978-1-58768-570-5 (ebook)
   1. God (Christianity)—Love. 2. Shame—Religious aspects—Christianity. I. Title.
   BT140.A9 2015
   231`.6—dc23
                                                                          2015015612

ISBN 978-0-8091-4961-2 (paperback)
ISBN 978-1-58768-570-5 (e-book)

Published by Paulist Press
997 Macarthur Boulevard
Mahwah, New Jersey 07430

www.paulistpress.com

Printed and bound in the
United States of America

To
Catherine Marie Kreta, CSJ,
and
Gerald L. McKevitt, SJ,
whose friendship and faithfulness
through the years
have embodied
God's unconditional love

CONTENTS

ACKNOWLEDGMENTS

What we present in this work reflects our research on the topic of shame and its corrosive impact on our spiritual and psychological development. But just as importantly, our theoretical reflections are rooted in our practice of psychotherapy and spiritual direction for over thirty-five years. We are grateful for the many people through the years who have given us the privilege of accompanying them on their journeys and for sharing so intimately with us. We are also grateful to our former students whose experiences and insights have enriched our understanding.

Inspiration for writing this book came from a chance, though graceful, encounter with someone we met when we were giving a weekend retreat at the Jesuit Retreat Center in Los Altos, California. In conversations that weekend and in the months that followed, our newfound friend, Christopher Tolk, a CPA and founding partner of an accounting firm in Aspen, Colorado, impressed us with his enthusiastic encouragement to continue our writing as a way of ministering to others on a broader scale. His aliveness as a person and his commitment to spreading the gospel deeply inspired us. For his encouragement and support, we are much indebted.

And finally, we want to thank Paul McMahon, our editor at Paulist Press, for his ongoing support and thoughtful editing.

W. W. A.
Loyola Marymount University
Los Angeles, California
N. C. A.
C. G. Jung Institute
Los Angeles, California

INTRODUCTION

When we decided to write a book about shame, we had no idea that this topic would evoke such enthusiasm among our friends, colleagues, and retreat participants. No one asked, "Why shame?" Nor was anyone disinterested. Instead, people said things such as, "Wow, I can really use that," or "I can hardly wait to read it," or "When will it be finished?"

We knew that shame was an important issue, but we did not realize the extent to which shame permeates peoples' lives. In the process of our research, we have discovered that shame is pervasive in our culture, but is frequently unrecognized, misunderstood, and misinterpreted. Furthermore, shame is considered to be the "master emotion," because it regulates our expression, even our recognition, of all other emotions, including shame itself. If, for example, we feel ashamed of emotions like anger, hurt, fear, or love, we are not likely to express them. If hurt feelings are shameful, but anger is acceptable, we tend to substitute anger when feeling hurt. If all emotions are shameful, they all will be almost completely repressed. Shame also plays a central role in conscience development and social morality and is used by society to enforce acceptable behavior. As the master emotion, shame hovers over all our social interactions so that much of our life experience is colored by shame—anticipating it, experiencing it, and managing it.

Most importantly for our work as therapist and spiritual director, we have come to believe that shame is at the heart of most emotional and spiritual struggles. In our own training, there was little mention of shame or even how to help people deal with it. We were taught to attend to emotions like anger, fear, hurt, and so on, but shame was bypassed, as if it were taboo. Only recently have social scientists realized that other emotions are often secondary, substituting for the primary, albeit humiliating, emotion of shame. If shame is the real culprit underlying much of human suffering—which we think it is—then it is important that we discover how shame affects our lives, keeping us from realizing our full potential and inhibiting our relationships with others, including God.

While there are many approaches to the healing and transformation of shame, we have chosen to focus on what Christian spirituality has to offer. That being said, we presume that readers will be mainly people whose Christian faith is central to their understanding of human life and spiritual growth. Although Christians are our intended audience, we think that anyone who believes in God—from whatever religious tradition—can find value in these pages.

Shame—the feeling that we are unworthy—seeps into everyone's life. All of us have feelings of inadequacy and secretly fear that there is something wrong with us, that we are not smart enough, not successful enough, not rich enough, not interesting enough, not good-looking enough, not good enough to be loved for who we are. Our goal in writing this book is to help people free themselves from shame by embracing their true identities as God's beloved. The healing and transformation of shame begin when we come to see ourselves through the lens of God's unconditional love rather than through the lens of shame.

"Look to [God], and be radiant," encourages the psalmist, "so your faces shall never be ashamed" (Ps 34:5). This biblical verse invites us to reflect on our images of God. Can you imagine yourself looking at God with the confidence that you will see God gazing at you with love? Or is your image of God such that you expect to see a shaming God, whose look is one of disappointment or disapproval? Perhaps you think that God is indifferent to you and ignores you. We have noticed that people often have two very different images of God: one that they verbally profess, and a second one that operates unconsciously and determines their feelings about God. The professed image is the one we were taught, for example, God is good, kind, and loving; the operative image is formed by our early relationships with God-figures in our lives, usu-ally our parents and close relatives. It is important to become con-scious of the images of God that are operative in our lives, because these images powerfully affect our sense of self and our relationship to God.

How can we take in God's gaze in such a way that our faces do not blush with shame? The image of God we present through-out this book is of a God who loves us unconditionally and desires that we be healed of crippling emotions such as shame. Using bib-lical stories, such as the bent-over woman in Luke's Gospel (13:10–13) and the woman caught in adultery in John's Gospel (8:3–11), we show how God's compassionate love flowed through the person of Jesus into the lives of people burdened with shame. Scripture provides more than enough evidence that Jesus' mission was to be the healing presence of God to everyone, particularly those who were outcasts. What was true for the people of Jesus' time is still true today. God's compassionate love is ours to relish if we but open ourselves to experience it. Joy and healing come, as the psalmist proclaims, when we can take in God's loving gaze and realize that we are good and worthy of love just as we are.

St. Ignatius of Loyola has given us a rich way of praying with scripture through the use of the imagination. Called Ignatian con-templation, it has led many to a more intimate relationship with Christ. Ignatian contemplation disposes us to meet the risen Jesus at the deepest level of our being, allowing our senses to channel the healing action of grace right into our hearts. Relying on our imagination, we immerse ourselves into a gospel mystery so totally that we are given an intimate, felt-knowledge of Jesus that goes far beyond the abstract and impersonal. This form of imaginative con-templation invites us to move directly into an event described in the gospel in order to experience it as if we were part of the event. Through such an immersion, the gospel event springs to life and becomes a happening in which we participate. Our imagination can transport us into a biblical story in a way that enables us to have a heartfelt experience of God's love. Through the power of

3

our imagination, we can actually experience the same kinds of healing as those described in biblical stories.

The testimony of countless Christians throughout the centuries is evidence of the spiritual transformation that imaginative prayer makes possible. Contemporary research on the brain also describes the power of the imagination to affect our experience. There is evidence that the brain responds to depictions of smells, textures, and movements as if they were the real things.[1] According to V. S. Ramachandran, director of the Center for Brain and Cognition at the University of California, San Diego, "mirror neurons are activated by the things we see and also activated when we simply *imagine* ourselves performing the action."[2] For example, if you imagine putting down what you're reading and going into the kitchen, slicing a lemon, and biting into it, you will experience the sensations of tasting a lemon even when doing so only in your imagination.

In a recent best-selling novel, *The Shack*, we find a vivid illustration of how the imagination can be a potent source of healing. *The Shack* recounts the personal journey of William Paul Young from shame and grief to healing and forgiveness. The story is told through the lives of the main characters, Mackenzie Phillips (Mack) and his youngest daughter, Missy, who goes missing, presumably abducted and murdered, during a family camping trip. Mack blames himself because he was the one taking care of Missy when she suddenly vanished. Following this unbearable loss, a black cloud of shame and resentment darkens his days. Life becomes a drab existence; a "great sadness" drains it of all joy. Then one day, Mack receives "a note from God" inviting him to meet at "the shack," the very place in the woods where his daughter died. What follows is a touching and colorful story of Mack's encounter with God. As Mack takes in God's consoling and unconditional love for him, his shame diminishes and slowly he is enabled to forgive both himself and his daughter's killer. The "shack" where Mack is invited to meet God is an image of that dark place in each of us that holds our painful emotions of guilt, anger, fear, regret, and resentment. It is a shameful place hidden so deep within that it seems beyond God's healing reach. Yet, it is precisely in this place of pain that Mack discovers the power of God's love to transform self-hatred into self-love and despair into hope.

During an interview before his presentation at a conference on shame, Young revealed his reason for writing the book. He talked about growing up with a distant and disapproving God whose expectations he could never satisfy. The oldest son of missionaries, he was sent at age six to boarding school, where he was emotionally and sexually abused. As a result, he suffered from shame so excruciating that he contemplated suicide. He was determined that his own children come to know the God that he only later discovered, the God of love, relationship, and mutuality. *The Shack*, which was originally written for Young's children, quickly became a best seller because it struck a chord among people of all denominations. It raises vital human questions about God, about life, and about suffering and forgiveness—questions that concern us all, such as the following:

How does God feel about us?
- How does the way God feels about us compare with how we feel about ourselves?
- Can God be found in the midst of our struggles with shame and other painful emotions?

How can we encounter God in a way that brings healing, forgiveness, and wholeness?

LETTING GOD'S LOVE
HEAL OUR SHAME

The Shack introduces some of the themes of this book. We want to illustrate how God's unconditional love meets us in our places of shame and darkness. We will show how the compassionate God, whom we see and experience in Jesus, is not indifferent to our pain, but rather invites each of us, like Mack, to a healing encounter with Divine Grace in our personal "shack." We will

discuss how distorted images—such as the judging God, the indifferent God, and the demanding God—keep us from approaching
the God revealed by Jesus. Because,

> Who wants to share their feelings of guilt and shame
> with a God who judges and punishes?
>
> Who can feel safe to unleash their anger and resent-
> ment about life's unfairness to a God who is lacking
> in compassion and understanding of human pain?
>
> Who wants to be vulnerable and honest about their
> mistakes and sins with a God who demands perfec-
> tion?

Images such as these undermine our relationships with God and
warp our relationships with others and ourselves.

While the Christian message has, sometimes, focused on a
fearful, wrathful God, there is a "new Christian narrative," which
emphasizes a God of unconditional love and acceptance. In her
book on evangelical spirituality, psychological anthropologist
T. M. Luhrmann describes this paradigm shift in the following way:
"In this new Christian narrative, the problem is human emotional
pain and the human's own self-blaming harshness—a kind of living hell—and the resolution of that pain is God's infinite and personal love that can be had now, today, as long as you truly accept
that God is loving; that God is present; and above all that God
loves *you*, just as you are, with all your pounds and pimples."[3] It is
our own self-critical condemnation, not God's judgment, that
causes our painful emotions. "God believes that we are worthwhile
and loves us for ourselves. We feel shameful and unworthy, because
we magnify our guilt and hold ourselves responsible for our pain. If
we really believed in God's love, we wouldn't feel that way."[4]

This book attempts to reinforce the new Christian narrative
that asserts without qualification that God's love is merciful; it is a
love "that reaches into the dark space of our flailing and our failing, our losing and our dying…[and] picks us up and holds us ten-
derly until we are healed."[5] God's love seeks to soften our troubled

hearts and to quiet the anxiety that drives our need to do every-thing just right. We need only to open ourselves to hear God's voice reassuring us, "I love you, no matter what!"

A contemporary writer poignantly illustrates what the love of God looks like. In a doctor's waiting room, she witnessed a young mother's love for her child confined to a wheelchair. Obviously dis-abled, the child could only squeal incoherently, and lacking all physical coordination, her legs floundered helplessly, her hands flung in all directions, and her eyes were unable to focus. Positioning the child's chair so that they faced each other directly, the mother began softly singing and gesturing the motions to "The Itsy Bitsy Spider" in order to attract the child's attention. Repeating it over and over, she would sometimes catch the child's hand and kiss it. Stroking her hair in a soothing way, she would look into the child's eyes and whisper, with enormous tenderness, "I love you."

> Is this how we are, I wondered, before our God who wants to love us just this tenderly? Our limbs flailing aimlessly, unable to unify our energies to respond to the gift of life we have been given; our eyes unable to focus on the love God tries over and over in so many ways to reveal to us; our voice unable to respond coherently to this God whom our minds cannot comprehend?[6]

THE JOURNEY FROM HEAD TO HEART

The Shack recounts one person's spiritual journey from merely believing the tenets of Christian faith in an intellectual way to profoundly experiencing the truths of faith in a life-changing way. Faith can come alive for us when the beliefs we hold in our heads make their slow way into our hearts, or according to John Henry Cardinal Newman, when notional knowledge becomes real. Belief in God's love is life-giving only when we feel it in our hearts. Spiritually, the longest journey that we must make is the eighteen inches between our heads and our hearts. Here is where the imagination can pave a pathway. It can bridge the gap between "knowing about" God's love and "feeling" it in the depths of our beings.

Through the practice of imaginative contemplation, it is our hope that this book will help you to open yourself to a deepening knowledge of God's unconditional love. May you experience the spiritual and emotional transformation that God desires for you and for each one of us.

CHAPTER ONE
THE CHALLENGE TO LOVING

"Shame is a soul-eating emotion."

—C. G. Jung

"Who told you that you were naked?" (Gen 3:11). This question posed by God to Adam and Eve represents a dramatic moment in human development, the onset of self-consciousness tinged with shame. Whereas they once took their nakedness as a natural condition, Adam and Eve felt it after this moment as a source of vulnerability, exposing aspects of themselves that they were anxious to hide. This biblical scene highlights a poignant shift in their awareness of themselves and their relationship with God, who created them and took delight in their goodness. It entailed a loss of innocence and a painful rift in what was formerly a relationship of closeness.

> They heard the sound of the LORD God walking in the garden at the time of the evening breeze, and the man and his wife hid themselves from the presence of the LORD God among the trees of the garden. But the LORD God called to the man, and said to him, "Where are you?" He said, "I heard the sound of you in the garden, and I was afraid, because I was naked; and I hid myself." (Gen 3:8–10)

The ease in relationship was now gone, replaced by shame and fear, feelings that distanced Adam and Eve from God and each other.

The "fall" of Adam and Eve has been used traditionally by Christians to explain our basic human condition as weakened and vulnerable to sin and death. As descendants of Adam and Eve, we have "inherited" the consequences of their fall and live with the burden of guilt and fragmentation, no longer enjoying the bliss of inner harmony and oneness with everything. Reflecting the message of St. Paul, Christians have traditionally viewed Jesus as the New Adam, who came to save us from the impaired condition of human life caused by the "original sin" of our first parents (see Rom 5:12–21). A Jesuit writer, however, has offered a new perspective on the saving role of Jesus, suggesting "original shame" as an alternative way of understanding the fall. He argues, "It might prove more constructive to view Jesus as coming to save humankind from shame rather than sin."[1] If salvation restores our sense of being whole and lovable in God's eyes, this creative shift in understanding can deepen our appreciation of Jesus' saving action on our behalf. By looking at Jesus' ministry of healing through the lens of saving people from shame, we hope to provide a fresh appreciation of Gospel stories as a source of encouragement and inspiration.

Shame and sin are, in fact, closely linked, in that shame is often the cause of our resistance to relationships. By inclining us to withdraw and hide, shame alienates us from others. It makes us feel safer to be alone or impersonal than to risk letting others know us. Staying hidden ensures that we will not be ridiculed or exposed. Spiritually, shame also makes us keep God at arm's length. It infuses our spiritual life with the fear that we are sinful and unlovable. Projecting our self-contempt onto God, we believe that even God will reject us. A graduate student in theology described her struggle with shame in a reflection paper. She writes,

> Self-doubt and reluctance to let God's light shine through are a pair of debilitating forces within me. I question if I'm smart enough to earn a Master's degree and to finish the program. I wonder if I'm good enough to be someone's wife and if I will be a good mother. Logically, my mind tells me that these doubts are groundless. I *do* have the abilities to do all these things.

I realize that my self-doubt stems from a deep feeling of unworthiness.

This student is atypical in that she recognizes how shame negatively influences her relationship with God and others. Sadly, many people are unaware of the role that shame plays in their lives.

SHADES OF SHAME

No one is a stranger to shame. We all know the sick feeling in the pit of the stomach that makes us cringe. A very painful emotion, shame is rooted in a deep-seated fear that we are flawed, inadequate, and unworthy of love. Shame makes us fear exposure, dreading that if we are seen and known for who we really are, we will be humiliated. Even worse, we will be rejected and abandoned. Although guilt and shame are often used interchangeably, they are distinct. Guilt is the feeling we have when we have done something we consider to be wrong. It is related to our actions. Shame, on the other hand, is connected to how we feel about who we are (our being) and not what we have done (our actions). Most people do not know why they feel ashamed; they just do. Therapists and spiritual directors often hear things like the following:

- "I feel embarrassed by how little I've done with my life."
- "I feel stupid and inferior when I compare myself with the people I work with."
- "My twenty-fifth class reunion is next month, but I can't show my face!"
- "I just cannot measure up to what a good wife/husband/parent should be."
- "I feel like a fraud."
- "Sometimes I act like I'm better than others, so they will think I'm important."

- "If people at church really knew me, they would be shocked by what I really think and feel."
- "I never feel like I live up to what is expected of me."
- "I think I was a disappointment to my parents."

"Not good enough" is the feeling that all these people have in common. Each of them lives with a nagging voice that reminds them over and over again that they are flawed and unworthy. We all have an inner critic that devalues us and makes us feel small; maybe not every day, but often enough so that we can relate to the self-doubt expressed in these statements. We do not need other people to make us feel ashamed. The way in which ordinary life circumstances subtly fuel feelings of shame is illustrated in the following poem:

SHAME
    This is the shame of the woman whose hand hides
    her smile because her teeth are so bad, not the grand
    self-hatred that leads some to razors or pills
    or swan dives off beautiful bridges however
    tragic that is. This is the shame of being yourself,
    of being ashamed of where you live and what
    your father's paycheck lets you eat and wear.
    This is the shame of the fat and the old,
    the unbearable blush of acne, the shame of having
    no lunch money and pretending you're not hungry.
    This is the shame of concealed sickness—diseases
    too expensive to afford that offer only their cold
    one-way ticket out. This is the shame of being ashamed,
    the self-disgust of the cheap wine drunk, the lassitude
    that makes junk accumulate, the shame that tells
    you there is another way to live but you are
    too dumb to find it. This is the real shame, the damned
    shame, the crying shame, the shame that's criminal,
    the shame of knowing words like "glory" are not

12

in your vocabulary though they litter the Bibles
you're still paying for. This is the shame of not
knowing how to read and pretending you do.
This is the shame that makes you afraid to leave your house,
the shame of food stamps at the supermarket when
the clerk shows impatience as you fumble with the change.
This is the shame of dirty underwear, the shame
of pretending your father works in an office
as God intended all men to do. This is the shame
of asking friends to let you off in front of the one
nice house in the neighborhood and waiting
in the shadows until they drive away before walking
to the gloom of your house. This is the shame
at the end of the mania for owning things, the shame
of no heat in winter, the shame of eating cat food,
the unholy shame of dreaming of a new house and car
and the shame of knowing how cheap such dreams are.[2]

THE POSITIVE DIMENSION OF SHAME

Not all shame is bad. When shame takes the form of modesty, for instance, it helps safeguard aspects of our intimate lives. It helps us to set healthy boundaries and to respect the boundaries of others, two important components of social relationships. Humility is another positive form of shame. Humility is our acceptance of our identity before God—finite and imperfect, yet good; weak and sinful, yet loved. We believe that God desired us into being, and we gratefully accept our dependence on God's love for our very existence. Pope Francis regards shame and humility as two sides of the same coin: "Shame is a Christian virtue, the virtue of humility."[3] Believing that it is appropriate to feel embarrassed or ashamed when we recognize our weaknesses and vices, he tells us that we need to stand before God "with confidence, even with joy, without masquerading....We must never masquerade before God. And shame is a virtue: 'blessed shame.' This is the virtue that Jesus asks of us: humility and meekness."

In a tribute paid to Pope Francis, Elton John said, "Francis is a miracle of humility in an era of vanity." Eric Clapton, an internationally renowned blues guitarist and rock star, speaks about the beginning of his prayer life and his surrender to God in terms of humility. Recalling the terror he felt as his second stay in an alcohol treatment center was coming to an end, he recounts the transformative moment in his recovery. "In complete despair," he fell to his knees.

> In the privacy of my room, I begged for help. I had no idea who I thought I was talking to, I just knew that I had come to the end of my tether. I had nothing left to fight with. Then I remembered what I had heard about surrender, something I thought I could never do, my pride just wouldn't allow it, but I knew that on my own I wasn't going to make it, so I asked for help, and getting down on my knees, I surrendered.[4]

Soon after this intense experience, he realized that something significant had happened in him. "I had found a place to turn to, a place I'd always known was there but never really wanted or needed, to believe in," he confides. "From that day until this, I have never failed to pray in the morning, on my knees, asking for help, and expressing my gratitude for my life and, most of all, for my sobriety. I choose to kneel because I feel I need to humble myself when I pray and with my ego, this is the most I can do.... In some way, in some form, my God was always there, but now I have learned to talk to him." Acknowledging the importance of a humble acceptance of our limitations and need for God, he concludes, "You are never more a mature adult than when you get down on your knees and bend humbly before something greater than yourself."[5]

SOURCES OF TOXIC SHAME

Our susceptibility to shame is directly related to the fact that we are vulnerable human beings with a wide range of needs and are dependent on other human beings. When our needs are acknowledged and honored, we feel worthy and effective; when they are ignored or dishonored, we feel powerless and ashamed. Theories of shame suggest that our propensity to feel shame, our shame-proneness, is developed early in life from a complex mixture of personal and social conditions. How prone we are to shame throughout our lives is largely determined by the intertwining of each of our unique temperaments at birth and the shaming experiences we endure during our formative years. What follows is an overview of common factors that give rise to shame:

Childhood Deprivation: Child psychologists have long known that early life conditions have lasting effects on a child's emotional and physical health. Young children are not only totally dependent on their parents for all their needs, but also highly sensitive to the feeling quality of the care they receive. It is not enough to take care of their physical needs; they must also experience unconditional love in order to develop into emotionally mature adults.

What do we mean by unconditional love? Unconditional love is shown in the way a parent holds, touches, and soothes an infant; it is shown in the loving gaze in the parent's eyes that acts as a mirror reflecting back that the child is precious and worthy; and it is shown in consistent care and attention that the infant can count on. Since infants and young children cannot communicate verbally, parents must figure out what they need and provide it. Parents who are well-attuned and emotionally bonded to a child learn how to detect what is needed and make the appropriate response. Eye contact, facial expression, holding, and verbal soothing are important aspects of unconditional love. When children are deprived of consistent and attentive care, they feel abandoned and become ashamed of having needs.

Parents do not intend to deprive or neglect their children. They are imperfect human beings who do the best they can with the resources they have. Psychoanalyst Donald Winnicott coined the term "good enough mother" to dispel the notion that parents must be perfect in order to raise healthy children. Rather, there is a continuum between adequate (good enough) parenting and inadequate (traumatic) parenting. Children can tolerate a certain amount of need frustration and still feel nurtured and loved. When the scale tips in the negative direction, deep feelings of shame and unworthiness can overshadow a child's self-identity, causing a lifelong proneness to shame.

Emotional deprivation in childhood can result from a variety of factors. Parents who were themselves emotionally wounded may be unable to give what they did not get. Depression and other serious illnesses can make the demands of parenthood overwhelming. Financial worries, the death of one's spouse, persistent marital strain, or divorce can divert parental attention from the child. Parents can also be incapacitated by alcohol or drug addiction or by fatigue from overwork. Any of these conditions can overshadow one's childhood, creating an environment that is focused on the needs of the parents rather than the needs of the child. No matter what the cause, when children are deprived of what they need, they blame themselves for being unworthy of their parents' attention and love.

Theologian Roberta Bondi illustrates this point when she writes about her experience of shame and self-blame in the wake of her parents' divorce:

> I could see now, rationally, that I had interpreted my father's leaving as a deliberate rejection of my love and myself as unworthy. I could actually recall deciding as a twelve-year-old that, if my father did not want the child I was, then I did not want her either. Even more terrible, I had discovered in myself, and I wept when I discovered it, that even as an adult I had continued to accept both the twelve-year-old's interpretation of what had happened with my parents' divorce and the twelve-year-old's scorn and hatred of that child she was as well.

I knew now that it was this—the sentence of scorn and hatred that child once and for all had passed on me—it was this that...was also at the root of my fears that by my unworthiness I would finally force all those I loved to leave me.[6]

Not Measuring Up to Parental Expectations: When parents' expectations are age-appropriate and based on the child's own unique capabilities, children can feel successful and proud of their accomplishments because their parents are proud of them. But sometimes parents have unrealistic expectations that a child be like someone else—a sibling, perhaps, or a neighbor's child—and when the child fails to measure up to these expectations, he or she feels ashamed. Parental expectations are couched in such statements as "You should be more like your brother—he always got A's"; "Why can't you behave the way that Mary does—her mother never has to tell her how to act?"; and "Other boys your age like to play football, why don't you?" Messages like these make a child feel inadequate.

Sharing the hurt and shame he felt when he sensed that he did not live up to his mother's expectations, a man writes, "I know my mother loved me, but that never stopped her from looking for opportunities to improve me. Unfortunately, although her intentions were good, such efforts were wasted on me as a kid. I always felt like she was never satisfied with how I was and that hurt a lot."[7] Another man describes his critical and disapproving father as "a highly responsible man afflicted by high anxiety, a violent temper, and a critical, demeaning tongue....Not knowing how to express his love directly, he expressed it indirectly in hard work, financial provision, and verbal demands and harangues, which left deep scars in both his children."[8]

Recalling the pain caused by her mother's disappointment in her and her sisters, a woman shares, "As a child I wondered how my mother could be so lacking in the art of mothering. Apparently, she was unable to see what was so obvious to all my siblings and me....The difficult truth is she was just as profoundly disappointed in herself that none of her daughters, though each attractive and clever in their own way, turned out to be [what] she had hoped for." She recalls that whenever her mother described a young woman in their community as really "nice," she felt an implied negative comparison to herself and her sisters. "The repeated refrain of disappointment with its predictable country twang of regret," she writes, "was sung in an aggrieved voice. If a happier tune of mothers and daughters thrummed quietly underneath it all, we rarely heard it. Instead, we were all caught up in a recurring loop of a dissonant *if only* filling the space between us."[9] She goes on to say that many years later, when she was able to let go of the myth of the "perfect mother," she came to see her mother as a gifted and intelligent woman "who struggled with loving well in the way all of us struggle to love others."[10] In Winnicott's words, her mother was "good enough."

Parental Over Control: Appropriate parental control involves setting age-appropriate rules and enforcing them with consistency. The younger the children, the more limits are necessary to protect them from harm. Excessive parental control, however, involves manipulating a child's emotions and independence to satisfy some need of the parent. Some overly controlling parents are perfectionists who want to micromanage their children's lives. Some are authoritarians, who believe that it is their role to dictate and the child's role to obey. Others need to keep their children dependent on them, so that they feel important and needed. Whatever the underlying motivation, overly controlling parents foster shame in their children by making them feel weak, incapable, needy, and dependent. Children of overly controlling parents tend to grow up with feelings of anxiety, incompetency, and worthlessness.

Sibling Favoritism and Sibling Rivalry: Children have a built-in radar that picks up signals that parents are playing favorites. Favoritism, whether imagined or real, causes shame because it makes a child feel unloved and inadequate. The two most important ways parents can show their love are through the attention and affirmation they provide. Ideally, parents love their children equally, but in reality, parents often feel more naturally connected to one child over another, based on such things as personality preferences and shared interests. Parental preference may also be the result of gender (favoring the same-sex or opposite-sex child), birth order (favoring the oldest or the baby), or how easy or difficult a child's temperament may be. Sometimes, parents feel the need to give more time and attention to a child with special needs. A parent's preferential treatment, real or imagined, can create jealousy, comparisons, and sibling rivalry. In addition, the natural differences between siblings can engender shame, as was the experience of a workshop participant.

> I have been unhappy with myself for many years and most of it comes down to low self-esteem due to being overweight. I did get lost a bit in the shadow of my siblings, especially my sister. She was the pretty and witty sister, my brother was outgoing and musically talented and I was always the quiet wallflower. What I lacked, I made up for academically. But the one area that always haunted me was my weight. I have never been skinny and have gone up and down since high school. My weight peaked when I was unhappy with my job and it was reflected in my weight gain. I was eating out of frustration and resentment, which then turned into depression. Having my mother comment on my weight did not help the situation.

How easy it is to feel "less than" when growing up with siblings who differ from oneself in natural endowments and gifts, and with parents who try to love all of their children equally while, at the same time, being sensitive to individual differences and needs.

Family Secrets: A family secret is the proverbial "skeleton in the closet," something hidden from the outside world in order to protect the family image. Family secrets can be about almost anything: mental illness, drug or alcohol addiction, sexual abuse, sexual orientation, illegitimate birth, suicide, marital discord, marital infidelity, divorce, unemployment, or financial struggles. Whatever the secret, parents caution their children not to talk about "it" out-side the family, because "it's no one else's business." What they really mean is "we will be disgraced if you tell anyone." The truth, how-ever, is that carefully guarded secrets compound, not lessen, shame.

Child Abuse (Physical, Sexual, Emotional, and Neglect): Child abuse is more common than most of us might realize. The belief that abuse only happens in certain kinds of families is a myth. Child abuse occurs at every socioeconomic level, across ethnic and cultural lines, within all religions, and at all levels of education. It can occur in any family, anywhere, and may not even be recognized as abuse, even to the children who are its victims.

What qualifies as child abuse? According to the U.S. Depart-ment of Health and Human Services, "'child abuse and neglect' means, at a minimum, any recent act or failure to act on the part of a parent or caretaker, which results in death, serious physical or emotional harm, sexual abuse or exploitation, or an act or failure to act which presents an imminent risk of serious harm."[11] Accord-ing to the agency, child abuse falls into four categories: (1) physi-cal abuse, (2) sexual abuse and exploitation, (3) emotional abuse or maltreatment, and (4) neglect.

The term *physical abuse* applies to any non-accidental injury to a child. This includes hitting, kicking, slapping, burning, pinch-ing, hair pulling, biting, choking, throwing, shoving, whipping, and paddling. *Sexual abuse* refers to any sexual act between an adult and a child, including pornography, exhibitionism, or secretly watching children undress or bathe. The term *emotional abuse* refers to anything that is harmful to a child's mental health, such as ignoring, yelling, screaming, name-calling, shaming, or telling children that they are "no good" and "should never have been born." *Neglect* refers to the failure to provide for a child's physical needs. This includes lack of supervision; inadequate shelter, food, or water; inappropriate clothing for the weather or season; aban-donment; denial of medical care; and inadequate hygiene. According to the US Department of Health and Human Services, neglect is the most common kind of child abuse today, accounting for three-quarters of the known incidents of child abuse.

Child abuse, in all its forms, causes severe emotional harm. It engenders shame, and if children blame themselves for the abuse, they may also feel dirty or stigmatized.

Negative Depictions of Sexuality: The way we are introduced to human sexuality as well as our personal sexual experiences largely determine how we feel about ourselves as sexual beings. From birth, children receive messages about their bodies and sexuality. Parents who are uncomfortable or ashamed of their own sexuality are often embarrassed by their child's sexual curiosity and convey the message that sex is bad and should not be talked about. Reflecting on her psychosexual development, a college student recalls how her negativity and shame began:

> Growing up in a very devout Catholic household, sex was never an open topic of conversation in my family. As a result, I assumed that "sex was bad." Since it couldn't be talked about, it was like a bad word, something that I shouldn't be aware of or have questions about. All through my adolescent years, I was in denial about my erotic feelings. It was as if sexual thoughts were taboo and if I were to even accept my erotic feelings, I was going to be punished by God. Later, however, I realized that repressing those feelings made me think about them more. Denial and repression are incredibly ineffective when it comes to sexuality!

Race and Gender: Racial minorities in all societies often experience the shame of being different; they may feel devalued and excluded by members of the dominant race. In parts of the United States, for example, prejudice against Blacks, Hispanics, Asians, and other racial groups is still felt, as complaints of job discrimination, police brutality, and racial profiling make clear. In China, the preference for boys and the suspicion of female infanticide dramatically illustrate how gender can be a source of shame. Religions are also guilty of inducing shame based on gender when they do not allow men and women to share equally in religious rituals, worship, and administrative responsibilities.

Socioeconomic Variables: Variables of class, education, and profession are also potential sources of shame. The deepening gap between rich and poor caused by income inequity and unequal access to education causes wide disparity in people's lifestyles. Poverty, unemployment, and homelessness are breeding grounds for shame. Being among the "have-nots" or the "working poor" engenders feelings of shame and incompetence, especially in a culture that often stigmatizes them as lazy, unmotivated, or stupid. In consumerist societies, marketing and advertising engender shame when they stir up envy and foster the belief that those who have more *are* more! People may amass huge amounts of debt to counteract their feelings of envy and shame.

A wide range of experiences can cause shame and make a person feel stigmatized. Although we have described the sources of shame separately, many of them overlap. And while much of the literature on the sources of shame focuses on parents, other influences such as "non-parental adults, siblings, peers, and the culture play significant roles as well."[12] Our overview of factors that generate shame is not exhaustive, but it makes the point that everyone is vulnerable to shame. Even those of us fortunate enough to grow up in "good enough" families, with "good enough" parents, can have pockets of shame that unconsciously influence aspects of our lives. Through no fault of our own, we are all susceptible to shame, and we must learn to deal with it in ways that are spiritually and emotionally healthy. As tempting as it is to avoid facing our shame, the rewards for doing so are many. Spiritually, dealing with shame can clear the debris that is in the way of our relationship with God. If at times our shame makes us feel unworthy of God's love and afraid to approach God, we can work on rejecting negative images of God that foster fear and keep us from experiencing God's unconditional love. Facing our shame also benefits us psychologically. The very act of naming, owning, and sharing our shame with God or a person we trust can free us from its power and enable us to gracefully integrate those aspects of ourselves that shame made us disown.

SHAME: THE SHAPER OF SYMPTOMS

Shame is called "the shaper of symptoms," because it takes many forms and wears many masks. Most of us will go to great lengths to hide whatever we are ashamed of, for we fear that we will be exposed and further shamed. The more shame-prone we are, the greater our need to keep others from seeing how unworthy and unlovable we are. We all have the tendency to put on a "false front" when we feel insecure or inadequate. We want to be seen in a good light, we want others to admire and respect us, and sometimes we want them to think we are better than we are. As human as this is, the real problem lies in believing that we are not "good enough" just as we are. Shame causes us to lose faith in ourselves, to believe that there is something fundamentally wrong with us, and to believe that unless we pretend to be someone other than who we are, people will find us out and reject us. These pretenses can take many forms, but they all have the same goal: to protect us from feeling shame and bolster our self-esteem.

Emotion substitution is a common defense against shame and one that is familiar to most of us. This is when we substitute a more acceptable emotion for a shameful emotion. For example, if I find anger easier to bear than hurt, I will express anger rather than acknowledge that I am hurt. If I cannot bear to be envious, my envy might hide behind a mask of grandiosity and contempt.

Perfectionism is a common mask for shame, especially for Christians who may equate goodness or holiness with being perfect. The reasoning of the perfectionist is that, by avoiding mistakes, one can be blameless and above reproach, thereby making oneself worthy of God's love and winning the admiration of others. Perfectionists avoid feelings of shame by striving to be flawless so that there is nothing to be ashamed of. And when they do make mistakes, they find someone else to blame.

Closely connected to perfectionism is *hypercriticism*. Being overly critical of others is a way of giving our shame away. It protects us from feelings of inferiority by substituting feelings of superiority. Pointing the finger of shame toward someone else temporarily relieves us of our own shame, as when we gossip. Another mask for shame is to *attack first*. Shame-prone people anticipate that others are going to humiliate them. A way to avoid being humiliated is to attack the person you perceive to be a threat before he or she can attack you.

Excessive caretaking is a familiar symptom of shame. While *caregiving* is rooted in a free and loving desire to aid others, *caretaking* has a compulsive and driven quality to it. Sometimes shame-prone persons become chronic caretakers, focused on the needs of others and ignoring their own neediness. They give to others what they themselves need, but are unable to acknowledge, because they are ashamed of having needs. Caretaking allows them to feel competent and self-sufficient, instead of dependent and needy. In this way, shame is replaced by virtue and altruism. People who are committed to lives of service in any of the helping professions are vulnerable to using work to compensate for feelings of unworthiness. Helping others can become a way of escaping from shame, if it becomes one's primary source of identity and self-esteem. Although caretakers are overly involved in the lives of others, they are often lonely and isolated in their private lives. Friendship and intimacy require a degree of open and honest self-revelation that is too great a risk for someone who is riddled with shame. The constant fear that others might discover who they really are makes being alone the only safe haven.

Additionally, serious health issues like addiction, eating disorders, depression, and suicide may be associated with shame. Much has been written about the factors that contribute to addictions and depression, and the link between these problems and repressed shame is gaining in popularity among health professionals.

HEALING BEGINS WITH FACING OUR SHAME

Identifying the sometimes-subtle defenses we use to avoid shame puts us on the path to healing, because the first step in dealing with painful emotions is recognizing them. Paying attention to our pretenses—the masks we wear and the ways that we try to boost our self-esteem and make others think highly of us—can be a helpful way of identifying our shame. Questions such as the following can also help us identify how shame manifests itself in our lives:

> What experiences can cause me to feel embarrassed or make me fear that I will be rejected or ridiculed?
> - When do I feel most vulnerable and ill at ease?
> - What feelings and emotions are unacceptable to me?
> When do I feel like hiding who I really am?

Adam and Eve's use of fig leaves to cover up what they deemed shameful reveals a twofold challenge: first, to resist the impulse to conceal who we are; and second, to accept ourselves as "good enough" with all our strengths and weaknesses, virtues and vices—good enough to be loved, without resorting to cover-ups and clever ways of hiding our limitations and flaws. Reflecting on her personal experience as a volunteer helping out at a special education dance class, Anne Lamott shares, "I will never know how hard it is to be developmentally disabled, but I do know the sorrow of being ordinary and that much of our life is spent doing the crazy mental arithmetic of how, at any given moment, we might improve, or at least disguise or present our defects and screw-ups in either more charming or more intimidating ways."[13]

The need to disguise who we are comes from the fear that something in us is deficient or defective. If people saw and knew us for what we really are like, an inner voice warns, they would be disappointed; they would not give us the love and approval we long for. The gospel message of God's unconditional love, however, challenges us to put aside our defenses and allow God to love us just as we are. This is not easy to do, since we are accustomed—in our insecurity and fear—to hiding behind our many pretenses. The word *pretense* comes from two Latin words: *pre*, meaning "in front of" or "before," and *tenere*, "to hold." A pretense is something we hold in front of us to keep others from seeing us as we really are. Pretenses, like fancy titles and designer labels, are meant to dazzle others in order to keep their eyes off our unadorned selves, which we fear are inadequate to attract the acceptance of others. Women's use of makeup can be an unhealthy pretense if it comes from a place of feeling ashamed or defective. With wit and insight, Lamott writes, "Joy is the best makeup. Joy and good lighting. If you ask me, lipstick is a good runner-up....I know women from every place on the makeup continuum: some who wear none...and some who wear a lot and look wonderful." Makeup is not a bad thing in itself; such things as tinted moisturizer, light blush, and lipstick can give us a happier face to bring into the world. "It's only when you think you need it to be concealed, because you're unacceptable, that makeup causes harm."[14]

THE STRUGGLE FOR SELF-ACCEPTANCE

To say yes to ourselves as good and worthy of love is a lifelong challenge. Reflecting on the human propensity for self-rejection, theologian Johannes Metz shares an insight into why God made self-love a commandment. "Knowing the temptation which humanity itself is," knowing how readily we try to flee the "harsh distress of the human situation," and "knowing how difficult it is to bear with ourselves, we can then understand why God had to prescribe 'self-love' as a virtue and one of the great commandments."[15] Growing in self-acceptance is not peripheral, but central, to the process of spiritual growth, because shame and self-hatred are psychological barriers to Christian love and service. Most importantly, self-acceptance is the foundation of our relationship with God. If we cannot say a grateful yes to who we are, we cannot say a grateful yes to God who created us. The ethical and religious scope of self-esteem and self-love is often overlooked. Understood correctly, one's yes to self "may be regarded as the 'categorical imperative' of the Christian faith: You shall lovingly accept the humanity entrusted to you!…You shall embrace yourself!"[16] Two major obstacles to self-acceptance are perfectionism and envy.

SHAME AND PERFECTIONISM

Earlier, we discussed how severe emotional deprivation in childhood is a source of shame. When we do not receive the parental affection we yearn for as children, we learn to hide our true self in order to win our parents' love and approval. Out of shame, we take on a false self to gain acceptance. This, according to psychoanalyst Karen Horney, is the root of perfectionism. Lifelong perfectionism, she theorizes, begins as a coping device adopted by children who feel emotionally deprived and attribute the lack of parental affection to their not being "good enough." To make up for deep feelings of shame and inadequacy, they replace the "not good enough" self with an "idealized self," which is capable of winning the approval and attention that they crave. This glorified self-image, endowed with inflated and unlimited powers, replaces the defective self-image. And, eventually, they come to identify with this grandiose image. Horney describes how this leads to the emergence of the "the tyranny of the should." This notion is a useful way of understanding the dynamics of perfectionism.

> The neurotic sets to work to mold himself into a supreme being of his own making. He holds before his soul his image of perfection and unconsciously tells himself: "Forget about the disgraceful creature you actually are; this is how you should be; and to be this idealized self is all that matters. You should be able to endure

everything, to understand everything, to like everybody, to be always productive"—to mention only a few of these inner dictates. Since they are inexorable, I call them "the tyranny of the should."[17]

Since childhood, we have been encouraged to abandon our true selves and remake ourselves into someone else's image. We have been admonished and pressured to be inauthentic and to mistrust our genuine feelings. "You are too sensitive. There's nothing to cry about. Don't get so angry. We don't do that in this family. You don't really care about that, do you? You must act more grown up." The message in all of these statements is, "We don't like you the way you are." Many of us learned early on that we shouldn't be ourselves and that others would tell us how to be. As an example of how this might happen to a child, imagine the following: A young boy has had a difficult and humiliating day at school because his classmates bullied him on the playground. Obviously upset, he tries to tell his father how hurt and afraid he was. Instead of acknowledging his son's pain in a sensitive way, the father dismisses his son's feelings and tells him he needs to be tough. He tells him that "boys will be boys," and that he should be strong and not be such a sissy. What the boy learns from this experience is that his feelings are wrong and that his father thinks he is weak. He feels ashamed of himself and is furious at his father for shaming him instead of comforting him. What he needed from his father was help dealing with his feelings; instead, he received a cold lecture that left his hurt feelings raw. He concludes that to win his father's approval, he has to toughen up, swallow his hurt and anger, and pretend that his father is right. Next time, he will remember that being vulnerable makes things worse and that it is safer and less humiliating to pretend he doesn't have feelings.

Even if our parents and teachers thought they were helping us, what they succeeded in doing was making us afraid to be ourselves. We believed them when they implied that we needed to be perfect if we wanted to be loved. Or that striving for excellence necessarily meant pursuing perfection. Many of us, as a result, still unconsciously believe that being perfect should be our goal. Although we may realize, on an intellectual level, that the pursuit of perfection does not bring happiness—that it is, in fact, a recipe for unhappiness—we are driven to keep trying. Spiritually and psychologically, perfectionism has a high cost. Spiritually, it deafens us to the good news that a loving and forgiving God accepts us in our imperfection. Psychologically, it compromises our integrity and undermines our efforts to grow in wholeness and integration.

Self-acceptance for Christians cannot be a selective process whereby some aspects of the self are claimed as good, while others are discarded as undesirable. For those of us who are self-rejecting perfectionists, the spiritual challenge is in embracing ourselves as we truly are; persons who are uniquely fashioned by God. In faith, we are called to believe that God's love for us is total and without regard for our flaws and limitations.

SHAME AND ENVY

Envy can also disrupt a peaceful acceptance of our lives. A friend who spends some time each day on Facebook recently described the envy that erupts in her when she reads that one of her friends is going on an African safari, another just bought a new luxury car, and another is celebrating her son's acceptance into Harvard. Suddenly, she is angry and resentful that their lives are better than hers. And then she feels ashamed that she is not good enough to have a son like that or the money to buy that car or take an exotic vacation. Before she knows it, she is on an emotional rollercoaster—angry, resentful, depressed, hostile, and ashamed. Envy has destroyed her peace and temporarily left her feeling shame and self-rejection.

Envy is a normal human emotion that we all feel from time to time. Benign envy motivates us to follow our dreams, pursue our desires, and take responsibility for fulfilling our needs, especially when going after what we want entails hard work and perseverance. As is true with all our emotional reactions, when we can acknowledge envy rather than deny it, accept it rather than reject it, we are able to reflect on what it is telling us about ourselves. The problem with envy is that it feels so terrible that our first instinct is to push it away. In contrast to benign envy, literature is filled with stories of malicious envy, including stories from the Bible like those of Cain and Abel or Joseph and his brothers. And while it is true that envy does not usually drive people to murder, it can be a destructive force in our lives when we don't deal with it constructively.

Spiritually, envy undermines our ability to appreciate and be grateful for who we are and for all the unearned blessings we have been given. The following account of a colleague whose life changed in the course of a weekend illustrates how envy can—without warning—upend the lives of ordinary people like ourselves. He describes his experience as being like an earthquake—sudden, unexpected, and destructive.

> Before I went to my college reunion, I was happy and content with my life. If you had asked me to describe my life, I would have said my life was great. My marriage was good, my wife was everything to me, my kids were doing well, I loved my job as an English professor. I had a healthy retirement fund, enough money to do the things we wanted, good friends, the whole American dream! But something happened in me that weekend that spoiled my contentment.
>
> When I got back, I felt down and in a real bad mood. I snapped at my wife for nothing. I couldn't stop thinking about some of my classmates and how successful they'd become. I started to compare myself to them. I compared my wife to theirs. Even their kids seemed better than mine, real high achievers. I started to compare everything. They were making more money, some talking about retiring in the next few years. I don't know if I can ever retire!
>
> A few times when I was there, I felt ashamed—of my life, myself, my kids, my wife. I resented them for not

being more like my buddies' wives and kids. I hate admitting this, because it sounds so bad. And then I felt ticked off at my buddies, like why should they get to have it all and I don't. It doesn't seem fair. I've worked hard and done everything right—don't I deserve to be happy? I guess it's true, nice guys finish last. I hope they all go bankrupt! I know I sound whiny, like a victim, but that's how I felt. In one weekend, my whole life seemed ruined. I was miserable.

Lucky for me, I saw my spiritual director that week. He got me back on track and helped me to see that I was caught in a web of envy, which made me miserable. He suggested that I revert my eyes from fixating on what others have, to looking more appreciatively at all that *I* have. His suggestion helped me to appreciate anew how good my own life is and to feel grateful for what I have. I know I need to work on accepting that life isn't perfect, and no one has it all. Yet, God has given me so much.

LETTING GOD LOVE US

We conclude this chapter with a beautiful poem written by a graduate student who has struggled for as long as she can remember with perfectionism and overwork. Newly wedded, she describes the slow transformation occurring in her—a gradual shifting from needing to earn another's love to receiving it as an unmerited gift. This shift is truly a movement of healing grace. As she grows in letting her husband love her just as she is, she will at the same time deepen her capacity to receive God's unconditional love—a love that radiates a delight that banishes all shame.

> *I'll let you love me when…*
> *When my face is painted and my nails are polished.*
> *When the bed is made and the laundry is folded.*

When my race is run and my jeans fit right.
When my flaws are gone and I've earned my worth.
I'll feel you love me when...

When I just wake up and you want a kiss.
When you laugh at me and I throw a fit.
When it all goes wrong and I'm still enough.
When I love who I am and accept what I'm not.
I'll never be
    Fixed
        Healed
            Perfect
                Done
I'll always be
    Held
        Wanted
            Yours
                Loved

SPIRITUAL EXERCISES AND REFLECTION

A. Reflecting on Our Own Experiences

God asked Adam and Eve, "Who told you that you were naked?" In a similar way, imagine God asking you, "And who told you that who you are is not enough?" What comes to mind as possible sources of shame in your life?

Shame caused Adam and Eve to use fig leaves to hide their nakedness. The fig leaf symbolizes the many ways we defend against our feelings of shame, vulnerability, and inadequacy. What are some ways that you find yourself "covering up" or "hiding" aspects of yourself?

B. Cherishing the Gift of Self

For it was you who formed my inward parts;
　you knit me together in my mother's womb.
I praise you, for I am fearfully and wonderfully made.
　Wonderful are your works;
that I know very well.

—Psalm 139:13–14

According to Ignatius of Loyola, our selves are the first gift of God to us, for each of us was "desired into being" at the moment of our creation. A grateful life must be rooted in a deep appreciation for the gift of life and a love of self that makes us turn to God, its loving source, with gratitude and love.

Shame prevents us from saying yes to the self that is wondrously and uniquely fashioned by God.

How would you assess your relationship to yourself?
Where is there peaceful acceptance and gratitude for who and how you are?
Where are you challenged to grow in self-acceptance?
Regarding personal limitations:
- Which are rooted in reality and invite your acceptance?
- Which allow for some improvement and invite your efforts to change?

PRAYER FOR SERENITY
God, give me the serenity to accept what I cannot change,
The courage to change what I can,
And the wisdom to know the difference. Amen.

CHAPTER TWO

IMAGING GOD, IMAGING SELF

"It took me fifty years to wipe the face of my father completely off the face of God."

—Wm. Paul Young[1]

"How does God feel about me?" If you were to ask yourself this question, what would be your spontaneous and honest response? How you think God feels about you is critically important, because it greatly affects the way you feel about yourself and the kind of relationship you have with God. Discovering who we are in light of who God is—this is, perhaps, the most important aspect of spiritual growth and transformation.

> Is God's love for us really unconditional in such a way that nothing can ever separate us from the love of God made visible in Christ? (see Rom 8:31–39)
> Or is God's love for us conditional, capable of fluctuation based on our behavior and attitudes?
> Does God regard us with disappointment or delight?
> Does God's love for us depend on our performing in ways that gain God's approval, or does God's love flow steadily into our lives, no matter what?

Your responses to these questions reflect your image of God.

BIBLICAL IMAGES

Our images of God are an important aspect of our psychological makeup, because they strongly influence how we feel about ourselves. The healing of shame must often begin with dismantling negative images of God that are destructive and shame inducing. Some of our negative images of God can be traced to the Bible. This is not surprising when we consider the nature of Sacred Scripture. While scripture is God's word, it is nevertheless recounted in human words. The Bible is a collection of books written by different authors, whose prose and poetry express their own particular experiences of God. Thus, it contains a variety of images of God that reflect the unique religious experiences of individual authors as well as their social and historical contexts. Among these biblical images, we find some negative and fearful, others positive and loving. This can leave us confused about what kind of relationship we can have with God.

According to Jesuit biblical scholar Antony Campbell, we have a choice among biblical images of God, and what we choose will make a vast difference in how we relate to God and live our lives. Theologically, we believe God is an illimitable Mystery, and is ultimately incomprehensible to our limited human minds. However, we have some knowledge of God, because we benefit from the gift of God's revelation, especially through the images contained in scripture. Using the metaphor of a playing field, Campbell suggests that we can view biblical images of God either on a level playing field or a tilted playing field. On a level playing field, all the images and metaphors of God that we can cull from scripture—judge, king, ruler, lover, benefactor, friend—"are given equal value, pointing toward what can be said of God, subverting each other, constantly reminding us of the limits and inadequacy of each, the tension between them disclosing the mystery." In contrast, on a tilted playing field, priority is given "to a primary metaphor for God, to which others are subordinated."

On one hand, living with a level-playing-field view of God has "the enormous practical advantage of a traditional view." With elements of the lover, the judge, the benefactor, and the ruler mixed together:

> We aren't constantly challenged; we just have to be found on the side of the angels at the end of life— keeping the rules basically. We can expect God to help us along the way, which is psychologically valuable even if it doesn't always come off. We know that being good is going to bring its reward and, perhaps even more sat-isfying, those who don't bother about goodness will get their appropriate come-uppance in due course.[2]

On the other hand, when priority is given to an unconditionally loving God on a tilted playing field, keeping the rules and staying out of trouble are insufficient. What matters is love.

> A loving God affirms a relational element in faith, invites a personal involvement. If I accept God's love, I'm accepting a relationship and taking on much more than just keeping rules. I won't be able to accept love for very long without returning it. If I return that love, I will be constantly looking to the beloved rather than to the rules. What will matter is how much I love, not what the rules allow me.[3]

Based on more than forty years of extensive academic and pastoral experience as a professor and priest, Campbell argues strongly that the primary metaphor should be of God as one who loves us unconditionally.[4] Thus, the image of God as Uncondi-tional Love trumps all other images. Put simply, his central point is that we can choose to view biblical images of God either on a level or a tilted playing field. Each choice results in dramatically differ-ent ways of living our faith. Ultimately, our choice rests on the question, "Which attitude to our relationship with God is going to enrich our lives most? That is the challenge we have to face, the basic choice before us in life," Campbell asserts. "What has bite for us is the question: What is the fullest way that we can live our lives?"[5] The importance of asking this question is reinforced by the findings of a palliative care nurse whose book *The Top Five Regrets of the Dying* describes how her life was transformed by what she learned from her work with the "dearly dying."[6] "I wish that I had let myself be happier" was one of the top five regrets. Many of her patients said that they did not realize until the end that happiness is a choice. They regretted that they had stayed stuck in old patterns and beliefs that were narrow and constricting, choosing to cling to what was safe and comfortable. Her message is clear—to live fully, we have to ask ourselves periodically, "Are there changes I need to make so that when I am dying I won't regret never having really lived?" If we apply this to our images of God, we might ask ourselves, "Is my image of God positive or negative, and how is this influencing the way I live my life?" If we discover that our image of God is negative and has a constricting influence on how we live, we can then ask, "How would my life be different if I were to choose a different image of God?"

There are important consequences to choosing to image God as unconditional love.[7] Because God's love is a free gift, we do not have to earn it. We only need to open ourselves to receive it. Because God's love is unconditional, we do not have to placate God like some kind of demanding or withholding parent. Negative images of God keep God at arm's length, as in the case of a woman who complained about her unsatisfying relationship with God: "I fear that somehow, if I really open myself to God, He will demand things of me that I don't want to give, and I will be unhappy again." Although she was earnest in her desire to feel closer to God, she had not yet dared to believe in a God whose love is unconditional and whose desire is her happiness.

A student writing about his strained relationship with God provides another example of how an image of God as unloving can be harmful. "I discovered that I did not see God as a loving, merciful God, but as a tester. Personally, I felt like God was always testing me. I never really felt like I was moving forward in my life, but rather was just surviving the hard times. I have been wondering for a long time if God was ever going to reveal to me why I had to endure so much pain and disappointment. Unfortunately, my image of God really instilled in me a lot of anger and confusion." He could not imagine his life as a gift from a loving God to be enjoyed as an opportunity for growing and maturing. Instead, life was one big endurance test administered by a God who was grading him.

Praying with her imagination on a passage of scripture helped a young woman discover why she saw God as a distant, impersonal authority figure, unconcerned with what mattered to her. After contemplating the story of the two blind men who cried out for help as Jesus passed by (see Matt 20:29–34), she confided, "I found myself being in the crowd trying to quiet the blind men. When Jesus turned around to comfort the blind men, Jesus turned out to be President Bush! In this imaginative contemplation, I discovered why I have always had a hard time approaching God. I realize the distance I have been placing between God and myself, because I do not want to be a bother. I have distanced myself from a personal relationship with God and placed God in a position of unreachable authority, much like a president." When we believe that our needs and concerns are too small for God to care about, we do not expect God to hear our prayers or to comfort us in our distress.

GOD AS UNCONDITIONAL LOVE

The New Testament repeats over and over again that God is love. The First Letter of John puts it most succinctly that God is *agape*, love understood as self-gift (4:8, 16). In words that strongly support Campbell's position, a contemporary theologian states that "*agape* is the fundamental Christian metaphor for the Mystery that is God."[8] This metaphor is fundamental to the New Testament and appears again and again in the core documents of the Christian tradition. Put simply by Simone Weil, "God is love in the same way that an emerald is green." This means that God is love through and through. Jesus compares the all-embracing love of God to the sun, which shines on the good and the bad, and the rain, which falls on the just and unjust (see Matt 5:43–48). This is how all-inclusive God's love is! "Why, then," asks Campbell in referring to his religious training growing up, "all the talk in liturgy and spirituality of being made worthy of God's love, of becoming acceptable in God's sight, and so on? What sense did that make if God already loved us?"[9] The Bible expresses clearly the central revelation of the Judeo-Christian faith: God chooses to be a God of unconditional love. Since God is Spirit, neither male nor female, scripture illustrates this unconditional love of God with both paternal and maternal images. By calling God "Father" or "Mother," the gospel proclaims that "the ultimate ground of reality is love" and that God is forever "for us." To acknowledge God as Father is "to become aware of oneself not as stranger, not as an outsider or alienated person, but as [one] who belongs or a person appointed to a marvelous destiny."[10]

PARABLE OF THE LOVING FATHER

Perhaps the best-known illustration Jesus gives us of the utterly loving nature of God is contained in the parable of the prodigal son (see Luke 15:11–32). The parable could be more aptly called the parable of the loving father, for it portrays God as a loving, forgiving, and affirming father. The father, though not in any way near death, takes no offense at his younger son's untimely request for his inheritance. Rather, he generously consents to his son's request and supports his desire to leave home in search of fulfillment. The parable likens human life to an unrestricted gift that we receive from the hands of a generous God. Like a loving parent, God gives us life and, without any trace of regret, freely permits us to live our own lives—even though our self-directed journeys, like that of the younger son, are sometimes misguided and our returns home often tortuous. The caring father kept his son in his heart throughout his absence from home and daily scanned the horizon for the slightest sign of his return. Then one day, he caught sight of his returning son, and even while he was still a long way off, the father was moved with compassion. "He ran and put his arms around him and kissed him." Startled, though relieved by his father's warm welcome, the returning son tried unsuccessfully to deliver the apology he had rehearsed: "Father, I am no longer worthy to be called your son; treat me like one of your hired hands." But his words—full of self-accusing shame—were muffled by a hug and drowned out by his father, shouting out orders to the servants. "Quick! Bring out the best robe and put it on him; put a ring on his finger and sandals on his feet. Bring the calf we have been fattening, and kill it; we will celebrate by having a feast, because this son of mine was dead and has come back to life; he was lost and is found." The father's magnanimous love, conveyed throughout the parable, is amplified in his exuberant response when his son returns. This parable encapsulates the stunning good news proclaimed by Jesus and leaves little doubt about the unconditional love of God, whom Jesus addressed as "*Abba*," loving "papa."

GOD AS A LOVING MOTHER

In the Old Testament, Hosea 11 stands out as a classical illustration of God's love for us. Considered a core Old Testament text, it "is frequently referred to as the Old Testament 'gospel,'" writes scripture scholar Helen Schungel-Straumann, who asserts that its "images have special theological power."[11] If we pay close attention to the images, she argues, the picture of God that emerges better fits the image of a mother than that of a father.

> When Israel was a child, I loved him,
>   and out of Egypt I called my son.
> The more I called them,
>   the more they went from me;
> they kept sacrificing to the Baals,
>   and offering incense to idols.

Yet it was I who taught Ephraim to walk,
   I took them up in my arms;
   but they did not know that I healed them.
I led them with cords of human kindness,
   with bands of love.
I was to them like those
   who lift infants to their cheeks.
   I bent down to them and fed them.

—verses 1–4

Although Hosea never uses the term *mother* in these verses, "he describes the daily acts and conduct of a mother raising a small child," notes Schungel-Straumann. Furthermore, the prophet states later that God "as a mother cannot find it in her heart to justly punish this child."

My heart within me is overwhelmed,
fever grips my inmost being.
I will not give rein to my fierce anger,
I will not destroy Ephraim again,
For I am God, not man
The Holy One in your midst,
And I shall not come to you in anger.

—verses 8–9 NJB

It is important to note that in the phrase "For I am God, not man," the Hebrew words used are *el* for "God" and *ish* for "man." While earlier commentaries have generally translated *ish* as "man" in the generic sense of being a human being, Schungel-Straumann notes that Hosea in this verse intends specifically to communicate "male" as opposed to "female." When the prophet wants to indicate humanity in an inclusive sense, he uses the word *adam*, as in verse 4 ("human ties"). Thus, she concludes:

If the essence of male (*ish*) conduct is justice, punishment, anger, consequence, then Yahweh's conduct is completely different, i.e., measurelessly without consequence!

42

Rather than being concerned with his pride, his rights or male "face-saving," Yahweh is concerned with saving his relationship, something which more frequently and strongly describes women than men.[12]

This textual interpretation relates in two key ways to our present discussion. First, it suggests that "God as mother" is also able to express Hosea's experience of God just as "God as father" can, as long as we are aware that both images, in their totality, do not exclude each other. Nevertheless, Schungel-Straumann argues convincingly that the female-maternal imagery in this chapter loses its "concrete expressive power if one presses it into a male mold."[13] Depending on circumstances, then, God can appear with different faces, this time as father, next as mother. While Hosea in other places refers to God as a jealous husband, apparently at the end of his long prophetic activity, he "questioned the meaningfulness of the male image of God. The metaphors of judge, king, shepherd, husband, no longer helped. Only in Yahweh's motherly love did the prophet still see a chance for Israel!"[14]

Second, Hosea 11 describes how God, though justifiably angry at the infidelity and sins of his people, chooses nevertheless to be a God of loving kindness and mercy rather than one of wrath and vengeance. This text clearly contradicts the stereotype of an Old Testament god who is angry and vindictive. Hosea's portrayal of the tender love of God as affectionately maternal provides another biblical insight into the nature of God's unconditional love. Along with Luke's story of the unflagging love of God as a father, it invites us to give preeminence to images of divine love, subordinating all other biblical images of God.

OUR IMAGE OF GOD REFLECTS OUR IMAGE OF SELF

"She would have been a different person if she had had a different God," lamented a woman about her recently deceased friend who lived a God-fearing, though severely repressed and unhappy, life. In her classic study of the psychic function of images of God, psychoanalyst Ana-Maria Rizzuto, MD, states that our God images influence how we perceive ourselves and others, and thus profoundly affect how we live our lives.[15] Consciously or not, how we picture and feel about God directly affects the way we picture and feel about ourselves. As Jungian psychoanalyst Ann Ulanov well states, images are "the language of the psyche" and "they touch our emotions as well as our thoughts; they reach down into our bodies as well as towards our ideas."[16] That is why reflecting on our images of God and the corresponding ways we image ourselves is so important when trying to open ourselves more fully to the flow of God's love.

Rizzutto maintains that everyone who grows up in a society where the symbol "God" is valued has a conscious or unconscious image of God. She is not claiming that everyone somehow privately or unconsciously believes in God, but that everyone, including nonbelievers, has some kind of representation of God.[17] Some self-proclaimed atheists, for example, can describe in detail the god that they do not believe in.[18] A college student's reflection illustrates Rizzutto's claim:

> During a class exercise, I stumbled on something that surprised me. We were asked to close our eyes and to allow an image to surface that would represent our image of God. At first, this exercise seemed pointless to me because I already knew my image of God—I did not have one.
>
> However, as I closed my eyes, I saw a bright light that struck me as a glorified being walking towards me. He stood surrounded by exquisite clouds in a beautiful, blue sky. He descended from the heavens with arms wide open to embrace me. A faint smile touched the corner of His lips, creating a warm, welcoming, and completely reassuring presence. At that moment, I felt His unlimited love for me. It was an overwhelming experience!

In processing this experience, she gained significant insights about her relationship with God. First, she uncovered an image of God that existed in her, but was not in her conscious awareness when she began the class exercise. At the start, she thought she had no image of God. Second, the image that spontaneously emerged into consciousness startled her by its unlimited love and warm embrace. She was baffled, because she had assumed that in rejecting the religion she was brought up in, she had at the same time alienated herself from God. Summarizing what she learned, she wrote, "This simple exercise deeply motivated me to root out my negative image in order to fully encounter God's love. In the process, I discovered my negative image stemmed from my struggle with religion. My negative image of God only existed on the surface of my mind and when I looked deeper into my heart, my soul accepted His love and guidance."

OUR IMAGES SHAPE OUR EXPERIENCES OF GOD

Our images of God influence our religious experiences because we meet God as the one whom we image God to be. Paying attention to our perceptions of God, therefore, is critically important for sound spiritual health and development. Through a perceptive, albeit nontraditional, commentary on the parable of the talents in the Gospel of Matthew (25:14–29), religious educator John Westerhoff makes clear the direct relationship between our images of God and our attitudes and choices in life.

As the story goes, a property owner about to go abroad summoned his hired help and entrusted them with his assets. To one, he gave five talents; to another, two; and to a third, he gave one. In his absence, the first two workers doubled the talents that they were responsible for managing. When the owner returned, he delighted in their twofold gain and praised them for being trustworthy. When the third worker returned only what he had received, the owner harshly criticized his performance. In his own defense, the third worker argued that the owner's reputation for being a harsh and demanding taskmaster made him so fearful that he buried the one talent in the ground for safekeeping. Calling him wicked and lazy, the owner complained that at the very least the worker could have deposited the talent in a bank and accrued some interest. "This parable about faith or perception," Westerhoff concludes, "confronts us with the subversive contention that the only God we are able to experience is the God we image."[19]

Departing from the more common understanding of this parable as a teaching regarding stewardship or the responsible use of our God-given talents and resources, Westerhoff's analysis underscores how our perceptions of God directly influence our behavior. Each of the workers in the parable, he points out, has a perception of God's nature and character that ultimately shapes his behavior. The first two workers see God positively, as understanding, generous, and kind. They invest their talents based on this perception. In contrast, the third worker's anxious and risk-averse behavior reflects his image of God as harsh, demanding, and critical. This negative view of God causes him to bury his talent, lest he incur the wrath of God by losing it. This creative interpretation finds support in perceptual psychology's central tenet that behavior is a function of perception. We know from perceptual psychology that our behavior is the direct result of how things seem to us at the moment we are acting.[20]

Each of us creates our own personalized and individualized image of God from interacting with others and learning about how our community perceives God.[21] Sometimes, our core image of God contains internal contradictions, as with a college student who wrote the following reflection: "My parents and teachers have painted God out to me as being a happy, loving, welcoming force. I feel like at times I can feel God's forgiveness and love when I do something wrong. My personal image of God is of a larger than life faceless figure that has the power to do anything he wants, but chooses only to love and cherish us all. My insight is that God loves us all and only wants the best for us, but he is the wrong guy to make mad!" We can see how an image like the one this student describes could keep him from living a free and spontaneous life, lest he risk making God mad!

OUR PROFESSED AND OPERATIVE IMAGES

Sometimes the image we verbally profess is not really the image that holds sway. It is not uncommon that our professed image (what we consciously believe and voice) deviates greatly from our operative image (the actual, de facto, image that influences our thoughts, feelings, and attitudes).[22] An experienced Jesuit retreat director provides a good example of this in recounting how prayer helped uncover a distorted image of God hidden in the cave of the unconscious.[23] Fred, considered a model Christian by all who knew him, was a young, dedicated professional, who also found time to contribute actively to civic and church organizations. He kept up an intelligent interest in theology and lived a simple lifestyle, rarely going out to eat and spending little on entertainment. He and his wife spent most of their vacations going to conferences and workshops. On one vacation, he decided to make an individually directed retreat. His Jesuit director encouraged him to pray by using his imagination to enter various gospel scenes as if they were occurring in the present and he were an actual participant. Dutifully, Fred followed this suggestion for prayer.

One day, he chose to pray over the wedding feast of Cana (see John 2:1–12) and discovered that this way of praying over a scriptural passage was easy for him. He was able to imagine the event quite vividly. Fred saw tables heaped with food, set out beneath a sunny blue sky. The mood was festive, the guests were dancing and the music was joyful. When asked by the retreat director, "Did you see Jesus?" he answered, "Yes." He then went on to describe Christ sitting upright on a hard-backed throne, garbed in a white robe, a staff in his hand, a crown of thorns on his head, with a disapproving look on his face. The appearance of this stern-looking Jesus at a fun-filled celebration jarred Fred into pondering what was being revealed to him in this prayer about his perception of Jesus.

This kind of imaginative contemplation, which will be discussed more fully in the next chapter, is a powerful way of hearing the word of God being addressed to us in the present. Like dream work, it can put us in contact with parts of ourselves that we have unconsciously repressed. When praying with our imaginations, we can be surprised by the sudden emergence of repressed aspects of our selves demanding attention. Such was the experience of Fred in this prayer experience, which revealed how his professed image of God clashed dramatically with his operative image. The image of Christ that surfaced spontaneously in his prayer revealed much to him about his basic image of God and of Christ, which had been previously hidden from him. Prior to this prayer experience, he probably would have professed that his God was a God of love, joy, and compassion. But deep down in his unconscious, another image of God was in fact influencing his life and choices. Reflecting on his image of a disapproving Christ, he began to understand why he had chosen to structure his life in such a dutiful, yet drab, way. The Christ of his contemplation was one who frowned on fun and demanded an unceasing application to "good works"; his was a severe Christ who did not allow the simple pleasures of life, like having a good time at a friend's wedding. He slowly admitted something that he had long suspected, but kept hidden in his heart: his numerous commitments to good works gave him no joy, but were driven by guilt and the fear of a demanding God. This discovery was initially very painful for Fred, but it was the graceful beginning of liberation from a tyrannical image of God.

RECOGNIZING DISTORTED IMAGES OF GOD

Fred's experience is not uncommon. Many of us are unconsciously influenced by negative images that compete with the image of God as unconditional love. Sometimes, these distorted images are the result of negative transference, the psychological process by which we unconsciously bring feelings from a past relationship into another relationship. Transference, for example, explains how people who were raised by overly controlling parents often end up with a distrustful and rebellious attitude toward all authority figures, including God, whom they perceive as domineering and oppressive, much like their own parents. In an imaginative prayer done in a graduate class, a woman was surprised to discover how her operative image of God differed from her professed image:

> When I closed my eyes and invited an image of God to surface on the screen of my consciousness, I experienced a shocking revelation. I remember first envisioning myself as a child walking through a seemingly enchanted forest. My surroundings were exquisite, including the warmth of the sun's rays shining through the lush trees, the bird's melodic chirping soothing my inner spirit, and the gentle breeze that flowed through my hair.
>
> In the distance ahead, there appeared to be a king's throne. I was able to see an ornate crown and long, purple, velvet robe that was adorned lavishly with threads of gold and precious jewels. At first glance, it was difficult, if not impossible, to decipher the face of the person sitting on the throne. It seems as if the staff, robe, and crown were floating in the air all the while forming the image of a person's body. Standing next to the throne was the image of Jesus that I had from childhood. He was wearing a white gown and had long hair and an overgrown beard. He had a peaceful and loving expression on his face, and motioned me with his hand to draw closer.
>
> I stepped forward with caution and felt extremely apprehensive. I wanted to embrace Jesus and feel the warmth of his love exuding from his body; however, the image in the throne frightened me. As I walked closer and closer, I saw the face of the image sitting in the

throne; it was my mother. I quickly opened my eyes and was stunned and disoriented.

I realized the magnitude of what I had discovered and knew that it would be life-changing. In the past, specifically in the work I have done deconstructing my image of God, I acknowledged on a conscious level my strict Catholic upbringing and my fears of disappointing authority, namely my mother. However, I did not recognize that deep within my unconscious, God and my mother were one and the same.

Recognizing her negative maternal transference onto God was a graceful moment in this woman's journey toward developing a more intimate relationship with God.

At times, our struggles to understand our present attitudes and feelings about God can be illuminated by reflecting on our past. For example, one man shared the following story with his spiritual director, which vividly illustrates how a distorted image of God can originate in a painful childhood experience:

I grew up in a small town in El Salvador where the church was the cornerstone of the community. As the church secretary, my grandfather was very active in church affairs. One day, he cut his forehead working in the fields. When I asked what had happened, he said that the priest had hit him with a stick. I was young at the time and my grandfather was not known to joke while sober, so I took his words seriously.

The next Sunday I did not walk to church with him. Instead, I waited until everyone had left and then I fetched his walking stick from the closet. I entered the church through the side entrance with the stick in my hand. I walked down the aisle in full view of everyone. When I was a few feet away from the priest, I raised the stick and readied myself to bring down my wrath onto a bewildered man. Suddenly, my uncle grabbed me from behind and whisked me outside. The priest was furious and banned me from church for two weeks.

My childhood blunder certainly hindered my religious growth for many years. After being scolded by the priest and banned from Mass, I started to fear the Church and the clergy. For a while, I strongly believed that God had created human beings in his image and then started to punish them when he realized they were far from perfect.

Today, I know that I was just transferring my negative feelings for the priest onto God. As a result, I stood before a God created out of the shame that I felt and the fear that I tried to hide. This was not the forgiving Jesus of the Gospel, but an image of a priest whom I hated.

Distorted images of God can also be the result of projection. Projection is a psychological defense mechanism by which people unconsciously disown or deny unwanted feelings, attitudes, and traits and assign them to others. It often stems from an underlying need to be perfect; to be free from any fault or flaw. And just as we project unwanted attitudes and emotions onto people, we also project them onto God. Speaking of this kind of projected image of God, J. B. Phillips states, "A harsh and puritanical society will project its dominant qualities and probably postulate a hard and puritanical god. A lax and easygoing society will probably produce a god with about as much moral authority as Father Christmas."[24] More recently, Donald McCullough illustrated how our projection-prone minds have created "manageable deities" or gods we can control.[25] These self-made diminutive gods betray our utter inability to comprehend the illimitable mystery of God. The psychological phenomenon of projection, therefore, opens us to the danger of imaging a god with attitudes, feelings, and traits like our own—and with the same blind spots.

An example of a distorted image of God based on projection can be seen in the myth of Prometheus, the legendary initiator of human culture. For stealing fire and sharing it with human beings,

Prometheus was banished by the gods, who feared the development of human beings as an encroachment. Setting God and human beings in opposition, the Promethean myth reveals how false gods are easily fabricated out of human projection. Prometheus felt obliged to steal what he could not do without because he believed that no god would freely give it to him. He was unable to conceive of such a god, because if he himself had been god, he would have needed fire for himself and would never have shared it with another. "He knew no god that was not an enemy," notes Thomas Merton, "because the gods he knew were only a little stronger than himself, and needed the fire as badly as he needed it."[26] Blinded by his own presuppositions, Prometheus failed to see that fire was his for the asking—a gift of the true God, who created it expressly for human beings. When negative images of God are the product of transference and projection, there is no possibility of developing a trusting and loving relationship with God.

DISTORTED IMAGES AND SPIRITUAL DESOLATION

If we are feeling sad and alienated from God—what Ignatius refers to as spiritual "desolation"—it is important to examine whether a distorted image of God may be the underlying cause. A West German study, for example, found that "belief in a wrathful God was positively associated with loneliness, while belief in a helpful God was negatively associated with loneliness."[27] In listening to people describe their struggles in relating to God, experienced spiritual directors often ask the following:

> How would you have to image God in order to feel the way that you do?

This question invites their directees to make explicit what may be giving rise to their feelings of distance and estrangement from God. The following are examples of responses this question might elicit:

"I feel guilty all the time when I think of God." This feeling indicates an image of God as someone who is a critical and harsh judge.

"I always feel that God is disappointed with me." This feeling points to an image of God as someone who expects perfection in everything we do.

"I feel that all the bad things that have been happening to me recently are God's way of punishing me." This feeling reflects an image of God as vindictive and revengeful.

"I feel that I can never do enough to satisfy God." This attitude stems from viewing God as a demanding parent, always needing to be pleased and placated.

"I feel that God won't let me live my life the way I want to." This feeling presupposes a God who has a predetermined blueprint for our lives, leaving no room for personal freedom and choice.

"I'm afraid of telling God what I really want, because I don't trust that he'll give it to me." This feeling of distrust points to an image of God as withholding and unsympathetic to our needs and desires.

Distorted images of God alienate us from God and leave us feeling guilty and ashamed. If your relationship with God seems distant and unsatisfying, taking a closer look at what you think and feel about God can provide insight into why this is the case. Intimacy with God is not possible when negative images and feelings make us afraid of being in God's presence. Becoming conscious of how we feel about God can help us discern the cause of our desolation.

In *The Spiritual Exercises* (no. 322), Ignatius provides three reasons why God may allow us to feel desolation—none of them having to do with a negative image of God. First, the desolation may be the result of our own poor efforts or laxness in using the spiritual disciplines that are needed to keep us aware of the presence of God in our daily lives. Ignatius believed that God always desires to be connected to us in love, but we may not be doing what it takes to be attuned to God's action. Second, God allows us to experience desolation in order to deepen and purify our love. The absence of tangible delight and satisfaction in prayer challenges us to seek the God of consolation, not the consolations of God. By being faithful to our relationship with God, even when feeling desolate, we show our desire to be more than "fair-weather friends." It demonstrates the depth of our commitment to God and expresses our desire for a relationship with God for itself and not just for the good feelings of consolation that come from the relationship. Third, desolation provides a contrasting experience that highlights the gift-nature of spiritual consolation. If we were to experience a continuous flow of pure consolation, we might be deluded into thinking that consolation results from our own spiritual efforts rather than from God's pure goodness and generosity. While in desolation, we experience our powerlessness to feel the consoling presence of God, despite all our sincere efforts. This inability brings us to a renewed appreciation of consolation as an unearned gift from God. Thus, for Ignatius, God can touch us with love and care through experiences of desolation, as well as through consolation.

REVISING UNHEALTHY IMAGES OF GOD

Psychoanalyst Rizzuto argues that our representations of God do not remain static and unchanging over our lifetimes. Fashioned in childhood and influenced by our experiences with our parents and early authority figures, they can be further elaborated, revised, refashioned, or rejected in ways related to the function they are called upon to serve at any given moment. Not only are our God images revisable, they may require change for the sake of healing and growth. How we relate to others is greatly dependent on our present perceptions of self and others, including God. Thus, we need to be conscious of how our perceptions are actually affecting our relationships. It is the belief of many Christian therapists "that God functions like a social relationship—a person—in a…[person's] emotional life and that any psychodynamic work they do with a Christian is essentially therapeutic work with that person's relationship with and conception of God."[28]

It is not uncommon to find adult Christians, who are highly educated and professionally competent, operating out of childhood images of God that do not reflect their adult levels of knowledge and maturity. Highly developed in other areas of growth, they seem to suffer a developmental lag when it comes to religious faith. "If the God representation is not revised to keep pace with changes in self-representation," Rizzuto rightly contends, "it soon becomes asynchronous and is experienced as ridiculous or irrelevant or, on the contrary, threatening or dangerous."[29] To grow spiritually, we have to let go of such outdated images. Just as we may be attached to a particular self-image, even when it is harmful or inhibiting, we can likewise cling to a harsh or stifling image of God. Letting go of something we have gotten used to can be unsettling, even threatening. We may feel resistant to giving up an image of God that justifies our present lifestyle or a particular pattern of behavior, fearing the changes that might result. Nevertheless, ongoing spiritual transformation requires a trustful willingness to let go of whatever hinders our relationships with God and others.

Revising old images of God in order to better resemble the biblical God of unconditional love can bring healing to those who suffer from painful emotions such as shame, unworthiness, guilt, and fear. Psychologically, such reimaging finds support in Rizzuto's claim that "those who are capable of mature religious belief renew their God representation to make it compatible with their emotional, conscious, and unconscious situation, as well as with their cognitive…development."[30] Theologically, this kind of revision is sound because "there is no way to avoid mystery in dealing with God. If we've got an exquisitely clear picture, then somehow we've got it exquisitely wrong.…An element in the mystery of God is our need to choose among our options for our God."[31] In the following chapter, we demonstrate how imaginative prayer with scripture can provide a space in which outdated and harmful images of God can be revised.

SPIRITUAL EXERCISES
AND REFLECTION

A. Window on God Exercise:
Clarifying Our Images of God

Purpose

To become more aware of the images of God that influence our feelings, behaviors, and life choices.

Process

Fold a sheet of paper once vertically and once horizontally to form four equal parts. The sheet should resemble an old-fashioned window with four panes.

> In the first "pane," draw symbols or words to express the image of God that has been presented or taught to you by parents, teachers, and friends.
>
> In the second pane, use symbols or words to draw the image of God you have formed from your own experiences or personal search. Here you might describe moments when you experienced God personally, whether in happy or difficult times.
>
> In the third pane, express the image of God that actually influences your feelings and behaviors, your choices and decisions.
>
> After finishing the three panes, study your page and note what the juxtaposition of the three images stirs up in you in terms of insights, questions, and feelings. For example, how does the image of God that actually impacts your feelings and behavior (your third pane) compare with what you acquired growing up (your first pane) and with what you discovered on your own through personal experience (your second pane)?

In the fourth pane, express how your images of God affect how you feel about yourself and your relationship with God.

Process Questions

When you have completed your window, reflect on what you have written down and ponder these questions:

When God thinks about you, how does God feel?
What is your operative image of God, as opposed to your professed image? Our professed images are what we say to ourselves and others; our operative images, often influencing us on an unconscious level, are the ones that actually shape our feelings and behavior.
Does your operative image help or hinder your self-esteem and self-acceptance?

Comments on the Exercise

The value of this exercise is that it can help us see how inconsistent we often are in the way we view God. At times, our images of God reflect the maturity of adult faith because they are based on personal religious experiences and thoughtful reflection. At other times, our conceptions of God are still influenced by the outdated notions of God that we acquired uncritically in early childhood and adolescence. Realization of this discrepancy can help us to "upgrade" our images of God in a way that enables us to enjoy and savor God's unconditional love.

B. What Gets in the Way of Accepting God's Love?

Reflecting on why we sometimes shy away from human intimacy can clue us in on why we may struggle to foster an intimate relationship with God and why the love of God can feel scary.[32]

Consider the following and ask yourself whether any such fear blocks you from a closer relationship with God:

Fear of being unworthy?
Fear of being dependent?
Fear of feeling indebted?
Fear of being found uninteresting or boring?
Fear of being vulnerable to rejection?
Fear of being hurt?
Fear of loss through separation or death?
Fear of losing myself to the other?
Fear that my beloved might want what I'm unwilling to
    give?
Ultimately, is lack of trust the basic block to intimacy?

CHAPTER THREE
SEEING WITH THE HEART

"And imagination is from God. It is part of the way we understand the world. I think it's okay to imagine God and grace the best you can. Some of the stuff we imagine engages and connects and calls for the very best in us to come out. Other imaginings disengage us and shut us down. My understanding is that you get to choose which of your thoughts to go with."

—Anne Lamott[1]

In our work in psychotherapy and spiritual direction, we have discovered the healing power of the imagination to reshape both our images of God and our images of self, and consequently, our relationship with God. A contemporary illustration of the imagination's potential to bring about spiritual and emotional transformation is the novel *The Shack*. A parable rather than a doctrinal treatise, this fictional tale has had a profound effect on millions of people who have been inspired by it to reconsider their negative images of God. *The Shack* is a moving account of how divine love brought healing and forgiveness to someone who was overwhelmed with grief, shame, and guilt. Through the use of the imagination, the reader journeys with Mack to that place of unspeakable pain and then witnesses his surprising encounter with the mystery of God's love. The author's imaginative depiction of the Trinity affectionately interacting with one another and with Mack gives the reader a concrete and inviting way of envisioning the Trinity. The transforming impact on Mack, and vicariously on readers, comes from a dramatic shift that moves the reader from an abstract understanding of the Trinity to an emotional appreciation of a God who is a community of interpersonal love—a love that overflows into human lives. As one spiritual writer rightly states, "The relationship between imagination and spirituality abides in the human heart, as the place of affective knowledge."[2]

Some critics object strongly to the nonbiblical description of the Trinity—God the father takes the form of an African American woman who calls herself Elousia; Papa, Jesus, is a Middle-Eastern carpenter; and the Spirit is an Asian woman named Sarayu. Despite this provocatively nontraditional depiction, *The Shack's* imaginative portrayal of God's unconditional love has deeply impacted many. Here are the comments of two such readers:

> It's a wonderful story of unconditional Love. Granted this book is a story made up by a man, God spoke to me many times as I read this book....It is biblical in that God is love, Jesus is the light and the way, and that the Holy Spirit guides us. This book does a terrific job of illustrating this....It is very thought provoking, and will lead you into a deeper loving relationship with God. Especially those who carry deep pain with them, as most of us do.

> This is a must read for anyone who feels stuck. This book changed my life. I don't care what anyone else says, God used this book as a tool to break the bondage of fear and guilt in my life. I have always loved God but kept Him at a distance because I could not truly accept His unconditional love for me....Even though I have spent many years studying the scriptures, I just could not sustain the joy He offered because I felt undeserving due to the abuse in my past. God's spirit penetrated my soul in such a way that I was finally able to accept His love to the fullest.

Through the door of the imagination, these readers and millions of others gained an affective and heartfelt experience of the good news proclaimed by the gospel: that they are loved by a God whose love is enduring and unconditional.

IMAGINATION AND SPIRITUAL GROWTH

The imagination has always received mixed reviews among Christians. Some believe that the imagination is not to be trusted because it leads to illusion and error. Others fear the imagination because it produces the "impure" thoughts that lead to sexual temptations. Still others, influenced by what was once widely taught in prayer manuals, believe that praying with the imagination is for beginners and must be abandoned in order to advance to higher mystical prayer. In this view, the imagination clutters the mind and prevents an intuitive awareness of God in darkness, beyond the domain of the senses. Written in the early 1920s, George Bernard Shaw's play *Saint Joan* captures the sense of suspicion with which the imagination has long been regarded.

> *Robert*: What did you mean when you said that St. Catherine and St. Margaret talked to you every day?
>
> *Joan*: They do.
>
> *Robert*: What are they like?
>
> *Joan*: (suddenly obstinate): I will tell nothing about that; they have not given me leave.
>
> *Robert*: But you actually see them; and they talk to you just as I am talking to you?
>
> *Joan*: No; it is quite different. I cannot tell you: you must not talk to me about my voices.
>
> *Robert*: How do you mean voices?
>
> *Joan*: I hear voices telling me what to do. They come from God.
>
> *Robert*: *They come from your imagination.*
>
> *Joan*: *Of course. That is how the messages of God come to us* [emphasis added].
>
> *Robert*: So God says you are to raise the siege of Orleans?[3]

While people will readily agree that the imagination contributes richly to the arts, its possible contribution to spirituality has been generally overlooked. Much of American society seems to have relegated the imagination to Disneyland and Hollywood!

Many contemporary writers, however, believe that the imagination plays an important role in spiritual and psychological development, and that it is a valuable way of knowing and gaining insight. "There is no life of the spirit without imagination," state Ann and Barry Ulanov, "yet people constantly belittle or trivialize it....Properly understood and pursued, the imagination is perhaps our most reliable way of bringing the world of the unconscious into some degree of consciousness and our best means of corresponding with the graces offered us in the life of the spirit."[4] As our capacity to see through the obvious to its underlying reality, the imagination gives us access to many levels of truth. It "does not separate us from the facts, but helps illumine the facts so that we can see more than meets the eye."[5] The notion of "thin places" in Celtic spirituality, for example, celebrates the transempirical presence of God that saturates all of reality. The divine presence is not perceptible to the human eye, but accessible to the soulful imagination. The imagination helps us to experience the presence of God, "to experience that which is not materially present...[and to] make what is absent to the senses present in the mind."[6] In this way, it enables us to experience ourselves as truly in relationship with an invisible presence.

SEEING WITH THE HEART

Imagination and spirituality both represent ways to enter into the mystery within and beyond human life. The imagination enables us to see with the heart. Thus, it is vitally important in spirituality, which "invites men and women into the world of mystery, the abode of God. The unveiling of mystery is always through some medium, either an image (God as Father or Mother), or a symbol (the holy Mount or the cross), or an analogy (the parables of Jesus, "The Kingdom of God is like…"), or a story (the Gospels themselves)."[7] The image of Christ on the cross, for example, can unveil the mystery of a God who so loved the world that he gave his only Son (see John 3:16). Gazing on the crucifix, the central symbol of Christian faith, is an ancient spiritual practice meant to deepen our appreciation of God's love—a love manifested in pain.

Many years ago, when Wilkie was in Kyoto studying Zen meditation, this practice of gazing on the crucifix was endorsed by an unlikely source, a Japanese Zen master. Yamada Roshi told him and his fellow Jesuits that the cross is the Christian koan and that contemplating it was a path to enlightenment. A Zen koan is a riddle or surd (e.g., "What is the sound of one hand clapping?") that baffles and stills the busy mind, so that an intuitive flash of truth can seize one's awareness. Excessive rational thinking, Yamada Roshi taught, gets in the way of grasping the mystery of God's love shrouded in the symbol of the cross. He insisted that enlightenment for Christians comes when they realize deeply that Christ on the cross is God's nonverbal proclamation of unconditional love. Such was the experience of Jesus' mother and the women who stood at the foot of the cross and understood its message of love. They witnessed Christ's pain, and in the words of "The Hand Song,"

> They knew it was love
> It was one they could understand.
> He was showing his love,
> and that's how he hurt his hands.[8]

The story contained in "The Hand Song" illustrates how images can trigger profound spiritual insight. Plucking off some roses from the garden, a young boy hands them to his mother. "Here, mama, these are for you!" Seeing the roses that she has been carefully tending cut off before she intended, she is momentarily startled, but accepts them with a smile. She notices some thorns buried deep in his outstretched hand and the tears that he cries as she gently tends his wounds.

And she knew it was love.
It was what she could understand.
He was showing his love,
and that's how he hurt his hands.

Soon after, the boy listens to his mother reading from the Bible as he sits on her lap. When he notices a picture of Jesus on the cross, he cries out, "Mama, he's got some scars just like me!"

And he knew it was love.
It was one he could understand.
He was showing his love,
And that's how he hurt his hands.

Zen enlightenment is often likened to recapturing our child-like consciousness, a way of penetrating a profound truth directly, unimpeded by the complexity of analysis. In the same vein, Jesus tells his disciples that they cannot fully grasp his message unless they become like a child (see Mark 9:36–37). Only grace can awaken our hearts to the profound truth of God's love manifested in the image of a suffering Jesus. Religious images, when gazed upon in a reverent and undefended way, can suddenly overwhelm us with a powerful sense of God's presence. At such moments, we feel deeply touched and know without doubt that God loves us dearly. Being so poignantly "struck by grace," as theologian Paul Tillich aptly put it, is how we as Christians experience enlightenment and transformation.

CHRISTIAN PRAYER: THE WAY OF IMAGES AND THE IMAGELESS WAY

Today, Christian spirituality clearly acknowledges the important contribution of the imagination to prayer and spiritual growth. The use of images is valued as a needed complement to an earlier contemplative tradition that stressed the inadequacy of the senses and imagination to grasp the mystery of God. Thus, the journey of prayer can follow along two distinct paths: the way of images, called the *kataphatic* tradition, and the imageless way, known as the *apophatic* approach. While Christians often value one approach over the other, holding both approaches to God in creative tension is important. Each can contribute to our relationship with God. Both traditions enrich our Christian faith and must be retained for the sake of balance and integrity. The apophatic tradition reminds us that God is always more than the human mind can ever conceive or imagine. Any real knowledge of God must be received as a gift of divine disclosure. As limited creatures, we can only bow in awe and adoration before the infinite mystery of God and wait to be visited. On the other hand, the kataphatic tradition reminds us how blessed we are that God has chosen to reveal God's self to us. The kataphatic approach emphasizes the use of images and words, especially those found in scripture, to transport us into the mysteries of faith. This approach affirms that divine self-disclosure has occurred in history and reached its high point in the person of Jesus Christ and his message.

The Bible is full of images that convey Jesus' understanding of the nature of God. In chapter 15 of Luke's Gospel, for example, God is likened to a faithful shepherd who cherishes the life of every single sheep in his flock, to a woman who values a lost coin so much that she stops her relentless search for it only when it is found, and to a father whose love for a lost son can only be seen as extravagant. These images convey some knowledge of what God is like. We realize that these images are not meant to be taken literally, for "in essence God's unlikeness to the corporal and spiritual finite world is total."[9] Yet, as analogies or metaphors, they communicate important truths about the mystery of God—how God loves and treasures each and every human being and desires no one to be kept from the divine embrace. The Christian God is not the faceless "unknown god" of the Areopagus (see Acts 17:23), but the person Jesus intimately addressed as *Abba*, loving Father. The Aramaic term *Abba* connotes all the warmth and familiarity of the terms *daddy* or *papa*. We have been invited by Jesus to address infinite mystery as *Abba*.

To maintain a healthy balance between the kataphatic and the apophatic in prayer, we need to move back and forth between using images in prayer on the one hand, and on the other hand acknowledging that our impoverished words and images can never be equated with the reality of God. Because our words—no matter how eloquent or poetic—are ultimately inadequate, we must regularly put aside our theological lexicon and approach the living God with open minds and dependent hearts. Together, the kataphatic and apophatic paths offer Christians a rich repertory of prayer methods. Although these ways to God are clearly distinct, they can both be part of our storehouse of prayer and used at alternative times.

IMAGINATION AND SAVORING SCRIPTURE

At a time when technology has sped up the pace of life, to savor anything we read might seem unrealistic and a thing of the past. Today, texts and emails seem to demand instant replies, and we are more accustomed to speed-reading and skimming than to savoring or dwelling thoughtfully on what we read. To read Sacred Scripture in a fruitful way, however, requires lingering with the biblical passages. Praying with scripture becomes life-giving when we engage the text leisurely, as we would an intimate conversation with a loved one. With an unhurried and receptive posture, we savor the moment and allow ourselves to be touched by what we read and experience. Using our imagination to pray with scripture slows us down, so that we can be nourished and moved by God's living word in scripture. By making the biblical text come to life, the imagination gives us a vivid sense of God's unconditional love made manifest in Jesus. The Bible is "inspired" in the sense that it contains within itself the power to evoke a deeply felt sense of God's loving presence. That is why it is a favorite source of Christian prayer.

A simple threefold method of praying with scripture is the following:

1. Read the passage with a disposition of faith and openness to the power of God's word. After a brief preparation to clear the mind of distraction and to focus the wandering heart, read the text slowly with a hunger for the spiritual nourishment contained there. For example, read the following verses:

   Are not two sparrows sold for a penny? Yet not one of them will fall to the ground apart from your Father. And even the hairs of your head are all counted. So do not be afraid. (Matt 10:29–31)

2. Dwell with the text, repeating a word, sentence, or phrase. Repetition allows the seed of God's word to sink into the inner soil of the soul.
   - Pay attention to what in the passage catches your attention and sparkles in your mind's eyes.
   - What images are evoked within you?
   - What feelings do these images stir up?

3. Either pray spontaneously or maintain a loving silence in response to what the word of God has stirred up in your heart.

When praying with the imagination, we do not need to have a running sequence of images. A single fixed image can move us to a consoling sense of God's presence. For example, the passage above may conjure up an image of God as the "Keeper of Fallen Hair." This single image, when allowed to inhabit our awareness, can fill us with a felt sense of how precious we are to God. Besides this single "fixed-frame" type of imaginative prayer, there is also imaginative prayer that is more discursive, like the sequence of a dream or a movie that involves characters, dialogue, and action.

IGNATIAN CONTEMPLATION OF SCRIPTURE

The method of Ignatian contemplation encourages imaginative prayer by inviting us to watch the unfolding of a biblical story,
seeing with our mind's eyes the individuals involved—their words,
actions, and feelings. For example, in contemplating a Gospel
scene, we move directly into the event and relive it as if it were our
own experience. This immersion allows the gospel event to spring
to life and become a lively happening in which we participate.
When we encounter Jesus this way, he is not a pale figure in a
book, but a vibrant person who draws us into a gospel mystery and
reveals its meaning for us in the context of our present life. T. M.
Luhrmann, in her study of Protestant evangelical piety, describes
the powerful impact that imaginative contemplation had on a
group of women who participated in Ignatius's Spiritual Exercises
with her:

> What astonished me was how intensely emotional the
> experience was. Every week when we gathered in our
> group, the women cried. They talked about their feel-
> ings—how moved they were, how frightened, how glad.
> They seemed rubbed raw by the time they spent in
> prayer. They wept about how much more intimate their
> relationship with God had become, how they felt his
> presence, how he had become more alive. All of them
> said that they knew Christ better: that before the exer-
> cises, their belief had been abstract—despite all [previ-
> ous] encouragement...to experience God personally....
> All of them reported that the exercises made God real
> for them in new ways.[10]

Those who find the idea of imaginative prayer difficult may
misunderstand the nature of the process. Thus, it is helpful to clarify a few points before moving to an explanation of how the
method works.

- Gospel contemplation does not require an ability on our part to imagine pictorially. For example, we do not have to have a vivid picture of Jesus saying good-bye to his mother at the start of his public ministry to imagine the tender feelings of this poignant farewell. Nor do we need to picture the scene of Jesus appearing to his mother after his resurrection to imagine the joy of their reunion. Although scripture provides no depiction of these events to help us visualize them, Ignatius felt that imagining these events would provide us with an intimate knowledge of the person of Jesus (*Spiritual Exercises*, nos. 273, 299).

  - Imagination, like an unused muscle, can grow just as our thinking does with exercise and practice. Our imaginations are not all alike. When reading a novel, for example, some are better able to imagine the physical looks and traits of the characters, while others are better able to picture the landscape and setting. Still others can imagine the novel's description of the smells of food coming from a kitchen or the sound of traffic at a busy intersection or the feelings of lovers on the brink of breakup. The imagination works differently for different people. Imaginative prayer can draw us into a Gospel story in whatever way our imaginations work.

- Further, imaginative contemplation of scripture does not require that we stick strictly to the gospel text as it is. Rather, the text is meant to be a story that frames our subjective engagement with the mystery and becomes a medium by which God can touch us in a personal way. It is not a canned or prefabricated experience, but a living, spontaneous unfolding of an encounter sparked by the text. Thus, imaginative prayer should not be controlled by the logical mind or by an anxious concern for a correct interpretation of the text. Imaginative contemplation is prayer, not textual interpretation. While critical exegesis is an important stage of understanding a text, scripture remains a *living* word capable of addressing us in the present only when we allow a "second naïveté" to reenchant it with the inspiration of the Spirit. If we are truly involved, the process will inevitably take on a life of its own, under the influence of grace.

When teaching this method of Ignatian contemplation, we rely on a procedure used by Gestalt therapists when working with dreams. The technique employed in Gestalt dream work contains three steps. First, the client is asked to narrate the contents of the dream just as he or she would in telling a story or recounting a past experience. Second, the client is asked to shift the narrative into the present tense and describe how the dream would be reenacted as if staging a play and giving direction to actors about how they should position themselves and what they should be doing and saying. Third, the client is asked to take the part of the different characters or aspects of the dream. This last step invites the client to fully identify with the people and actions contained in the dream.

Dramatization is essential to Gestalt therapy's approach to dreams. The one working on a dream reenacts it by alternately playing out its different parts. Normally, several chairs are used and the client shuttles back and forth between them as different parts of the conflict are enacted. The client may first play his overbearing conscience (what Fritz Perls, the founder of Gestalt Therapy, labeled the "top dog") and yell at an imaginary self in the other chair to do better. Then switching chairs, the client will be the submissive, whining, yet obstinate and wily "underdog," who limps through life spitefully defying his conscience. The point, of course, is that both parts are really the client himself, though each is trapped in a struggle against the other. By getting the client to give each part its say, he is led to the realization that, despite his experience of fragmentation, he is only one organism.

An important goal of Gestalt therapy is to help the client achieve greater wholeness by reintegrating aspects of the self that have been divorced from consciousness. According to Gestalt therapy, each element of a dream represents a disowned fragment of one's personality. For example, an angry and violent character in a dream suggests that the client's feelings of anger and violence are being repressed. Or, a taken-for-granted and trampled doormat in a dream may help the client, while identifying with that mat, get in touch with feelings of being abused and unappreciated. This three-step approach of Gestalt dream work is helpful for someone learning how to practice Ignatian contemplation. By applying the same three steps to contemplating a biblical event, we can achieve a progressively deeper immersion into a mystery of faith. What follows is an application of this Gestalt procedure to praying with scripture:

> *First,* read the account of an event or mystery in scripture, like the story of how the "good thief" crucified next to Jesus received the healing and merciful love of God before he died (see Luke 23:39–43).
>
> *Second,* identify with one of the onlookers and describe the event from his or her point of view. Do this as if the event were actually unfolding right now in front of your eyes. See an example of this kind of onlooker's account in our imaginative description of "the good thief's" final moments as recounted by his younger brother.

The Good Thief (*Luke 23:39–43*)

A criminal crucified next to Jesus is known to the world as "the good thief." But to me, he was "Josh," my big brother. Growing up, we were never really close, but we shared the same small bedroom until I was six years old. In mom's eyes, Josh was a good boy by nature, but was ruined by my father's alcoholic rage, which was for whatever reason always directed at Josh. Josh's life was made miserable by years of physical and emotional abuse from dad. To escape, Josh increasingly stayed away from home—until one day, he completely disappeared from our lives. Seeing the sad confusion in my young face, my mother drew me close and gently told me that Josh had been arrested and imprisoned for killing a man in the process of a robbery. Then, when he never returned home after he served his time, mom shared that he had fallen in with a gang of thieves and would always either be on the run or in prison.

So, it happened that I was there at the place called the Skull when Jesus of Nazareth was put to death. Josh and another criminal were hanging on crosses on either side of Jesus. I was the only family member there to witness this sad ending to Josh's troubled life. I felt that it was important that someone should represent the family, but I was afraid of the jeering, angry mob. Wanting to be unnoticed, I nervously blended in with the crowd, hoping that my brother would spot me and not feel so desperately alone.

What I witnessed that day gave me such peace and comfort. The criminal on the opposite side of Josh was mocking Jesus and taunting him about his powerlessness. Then I heard Josh telling the thief who was shaming Jesus to shut up, because Jesus, unlike the two of them, did not deserve the harsh punishment he was receiving. He was innocent; they were guilty. After this, Josh turned to Jesus and asked for reassurance as he faced death. The compassionate look on Jesus' face and his words of tender mercy lifted Josh's spirit. I could tell by the peaceful look on my brother's face. I heard Jesus reassure Josh that he was forgiven and would be okay. Jesus promised him that from that day on, they would be together in the presence of God.

This experience on the day that my brother Josh was executed has remained indelibly in my heart and grounds my faith in God's compassionate love for all—no matter what.

Third, insert yourself into the event by identifying with
one of the active participants in the scene. As you
experience what is happening in the gospel scene, be
aware of what you are thinking, sensing, and feeling—your entire subjective response.

The words of the late theologian William Spohn capture the value
of contemplating scripture through the method of imaginative
identification with gospel characters:

As we tangibly and visually move into their narrated
encounter with the Lord, we find in ourselves some
echo of their response: If Peter could be forgiven, so can
I. If the father could welcome home the prodigal son,
then my fears of God's anger are without foundation.
We learn to "ask for what we want" in these contem-
plations by the example of these characters in the story.
They raise our expectations and open us to hear the
Lord's words to us today.[11]

The value of this approach is that it can immerse us so deeply
into a gospel mystery that we get caught up in a personal encounter
with the risen Jesus. As often happens in a psychodrama or a play,
there can come a time in contemplation when the artificiality of the
put-on identity slips away and the gospel character comes to life in
us. For example, when identifying with the blind beggar, Bartimaeus,
in Mark's Gospel (10:46–52), we might suddenly experience a shift,
and then it is no longer Bartimaeus the blind beggar who is being
summoned to Jesus and being healed. It is the blind part of us that is
being led out of the darkness of personal confusion by the Lord's
healing touch. It is no longer Bartimaeus who is crying out with
desperation for help, but a desperately blind part of us that seeks
enlightenment—a part of us, for example, that is blind to what is
happening in a valued relationship threatened by months of icy
silence or is blind to effective ways of communicating with a
teenage child who is depressed. When our contemplation shifts

from imaginative role-playing to spontaneous identification, we are drawn into a graced encounter with the risen Christ today. An important value of Ignatian contemplation is that it trains us to spot the "rhyme"—the similarities that exist between biblical narratives and our own lives. By helping us identify the analogy between the two, we move from the memory of God's intervention in the past to the recognition of God's action in our present lives.[12]

Ignatian contemplation is similar to "active imagination," a meditative, dialogic process developed by Carl Jung as an adjunct to dream work. A useful technique that can be adapted to many different situations, active imagination, like Gestalt therapy, involves interacting with aspects of ourselves that have been disowned. Jung discovered that our engagement with images that are evoked by internal voices and moods can bring about positive changes. A key to this process of active imagination is allowing the inner images to spontaneously unfold and to speak for themselves, without imposing our agendas. Jung strongly encourages us to personally respond to the drama that is being enacted. In his words, "You yourself must enter into the process with your personal reactions…as if the drama being enacted before your eyes were real."[13] The goal of active imagination is to foster greater wholeness and integration.

Like Gestalt dream therapy and Jungian active imagination, Ignatian contemplation can help connect us with wounded and disowned parts of ourselves. The journey toward healing and wholeness is fostered by prayer when it opens us to God's compassionate presence. Those who practice Ignatian contemplation are often surprised by what emerges in the safety of prayer:

> The frightened inner child can drop the pretense of worldly self-sufficiency and hear the Lord say, "Do not fear, for I am with you" (Isa 43:5).
> The chronic worrier of sleepless nights can find consolation in the Lord's assurance, "Do not be afraid, little flock, for it is your Father's good pleasure to give you the kingdom" (Luke 12:32).

The sexually compulsive part can be relieved of its shame and confusion by the unconditional acceptance of Jesus, who says to it what he said to the adulterous woman, "Has no one condemned you?... Neither do I condemn you" (John 8:10–11).

The cold and embittered self can have hope in God's promise that "a new heart I will give you, and a new spirit I will put within you; and I will remove from your body the heart of stone and give you a heart of flesh" (Ezek 36:26–27).

By allowing these parts to approach the risen Jesus in the intimacy of prayer, Ignatian contemplation can bring about a powerfully transforming encounter with the living word of God. While a fear of painful exposure can cause us to resist or shun a direct confrontation with God in prayer, scriptural stories can provide a safe medium for allowing divine access to the vulnerable parts of us that need God's healing. In group therapy, the technique of role-playing is sometimes used to help a person inhibited by shame to own such negative feelings as fear or anger. By identifying with a character caught up in fear or rage, for example, role-playing allows one to feel and express these painful feelings as if they were someone else's. Sometimes this pretending, when uninhibited and spontaneous, actually triggers one's own authentic feelings. Surfacing previously buried feelings allows a process of healing to begin. Imaginative prayer with scripture can function in a similar way.

IMAGINATIVE PRAYER AS "TRANSITIONAL SPACE"

Praying with the imagination can do for us what play does for a child. Play occurs in what British psychoanalyst D. W. Winnicott called the "intermediate area of experiencing," an area between the subjective mind and the external world. Here the child in imaginative play can experience a "transitional object," a concrete object that helps the child to tolerate being away from the mother. Transitional objects enable the child to stay emotionally connected to the absent mother by providing something that is tangible and perceptible, like a teddy bear, a furry bunny, or a favorite blanket. Transitional objects, according to Winnicott, allow the child to hold on to what is good in the mother when the mother is gone.

In a similar way, biblical images and stories can serve as "transitional objects" that connect us with the real, though imperceptible, presence of God. While we believe that God is always present, we rely on our practice of prayer to increase our awareness of God in our lives. Dwelling with biblical images, stories, and symbols can help us stay connected to the intangible presence of God in the way that a child's teddy bear or favorite blanket can help the child stay connected to the mother when she is not physically present.[14] Of course, to experience God's presence is always a gift that we receive, not something we can make happen through our own efforts. As Jesus instructed Nicodemus in their nighttime rendezvous, the Spirit is like the mysterious wind, which "blows wherever it pleases." We cannot create the wind nor can we control it. All we can do is to set up the sails of our lives so that when the wind of the Spirit enters, we can receive it. Thus, St. Augustine taught long ago that setting the sails through our efforts at prayer is our part; sending the wind is God's. Abetted by grace, praying with our imaginations can enable us to experience God's presence in a tangible way. We recognize these moments as grace-filled because they are accompanied by an increase of faith, hope, love, and consoling feelings of peace, love, and joy.

Prayer as transitional space allows us to imagine, in new and vivid ways, the intimacy and friendship with God that our Christian faith calls us to. Images that arise from praying with scripture enlarge our vision of what is possible for a fuller life and bridge our present realities with future possibilities.[15] Writing about the transformational power of imaginative prayer, Jesuit poet Patrick Purnell states, "Imagination is at the heart of conversion.

We change, not because of doctrinal argument or moral persuasion, though both have their place, but because the imagination calls us into a new future and offers us an incentive to change. Imagination offers us images and pictures of how the pieces of our lives could fit together in a completely new way."[16]

CHAPTER FOUR
JESUS AS THE COMPASSION OF GOD

Jesus "is the image of the invisible God."
—Colossians 1:15

Central to the healing of shame is the ability to feel our pain and simultaneously to feel God's compassionate love for us. Contemplating the life of Jesus and noticing his compassionate response to human suffering gets us in touch with God's loving nature, because Jesus "is the image of the invisible God." The incarnation is the cornerstone of Christian faith. As Christians, we believe that Jesus is the divine Word, who took on human flesh and revealed the mystery of God. "No one has ever seen God," writes the evangelist John. "It is God the only Son, who is close to the Father's heart, who has made him known" (John 1:18). This is the *good news*, that we have access to some knowledge of the illimitable mystery of God through Christ, who is "the image of the invisible God" (Col 1:15). Writing about the incarnation, contemporary biblical scholar Marcus Borg emphasizes that Jesus is "the decisive disclosure and epiphany of what can be seen of God embodied in a human life."[1] For Christians, the pathway to God is through understanding the meaning and message of Jesus.

JESUS, THE COMPASSION OF GOD

To bear witness to a God of unconditional love—this, Jesus knew in a profound way, was his life's work. Jesus came to this self-defining realization after reflecting on the message of John the Baptist and arriving at his own conviction about God's attitude toward humankind. He rejected the forbidding ascetical image, which characterized the Baptist's message, because in his heart "already lived the God of love and the love of God instead of the God of judgment," wrath, and retribution conceived by John.[2] This is the central thesis of Shusaku Endo's A Life of Jesus, which received wide acclaim for its "stunning interpretation of scriptural events, based on solid research...and a trusted intuition."[3] The image of Jesus we propose here follows the contours of Endo's portrait.

The stark contrast between John the Baptist and Jesus lay not only in the tone of each man's speech, but more importantly in how each imaged God. Austerely clothed in a camel hair garment tied at the waist by a leather strap, John preached repentance. Warning of God's wrath toward the complacent "brood of vipers" who felt no need for reform, John projected an image of God that resembled that of a punishing father. Jesus' image of God, however, reflected his firsthand experience of the suffering of those around him—like the people in his little town of Nazareth who lived in poverty and squalor and who, like the lepers, prostitutes, and tax collectors, were burdened by sickness, shame, and rejection. Intuitively, he knew that what people needed was to know that God loved them unconditionally and cared about their suffering. His heart, moved by compassion, fashioned an image of God that is like a gentle and caring mother, rather than a stern and angry father. The tender concern of Jesus for those who were tired and oppressed resounds in his invitation to find relief in him: "Come to me, all you that are weary and are carrying heavy burdens, and I will give you rest. Take my yoke upon you, and learn from me; for I am gentle and humble in heart, *and you will find rest for your souls*" (Matt 11:28–30, emphasis added).

A MATERNAL IMAGE OF GOD

In the preface to the U.S. edition of his A Life of Jesus, Endo explains his rationale for presenting a maternal image of God.

Originally writing for a Japanese audience, Endo, himself a Christian, sought to portray Jesus in a way that would be most understandable to the psychology of his readers and attuned with their religious sensibilities. Because the religious mentality of the Japanese is responsive to one who "suffers with us" and who "allows for our weakness," it cannot accept the notion of a God who judges humans harshly and then punishes them. "With this fact in mind," explains Endo, "I tried not so much to depict God in the father-image that tends to characterize Christianity, but rather to depict the kind-hearted maternal aspect of God revealed to us in the personality of Jesus."[4]

Endo's focus on the maternal aspect of God manifested in Jesus echoes the revelation of Julian of Norwich, a fourteenth-century English mystic, who referred to Jesus as Mother. Julian speaks in paradoxical terms of "our precious Mother Jesus," who protects and strengthens us. "Our savior is our true Mother," she writes, "in whom we are endlessly born and out of whom we shall never come."[5] This maternal care never leaves us: "The sweet gracious hands of our Mother are ready and diligent about us," like a caring nurse who attends to the safety of her child.[6] Julian uses womb-like images to express her deep sense of God's intimate, encompassing, and secure love. We are "enclosed" in the community of the Trinity;[7] God is "our clothing, who wraps and enfolds us for love, embraces and shelters us, surrounds us for his love."[8] These feminine images serve as lenses through which Julian sees God and God's affectionate relationship with us. Julian's appreciation of God's maternal love finds strong resonance today in both Endo's *A Life of Jesus* and in the image of Jesus we present here.

Of course, a balanced understanding of Jesus requires us to consider that Jesus was able to integrate both the masculine (*animus*) and the feminine (*anima*) in his human development. In terms of masculine development, for example, Jesus was assertive and strong in his unswerving commitment to his calling to embody the merciful love of God for all. We see this aspect of Jesus clearly in the beginning of Luke's journey section, which states that Jesus "set his face to go to Jerusalem" (Luke 9:51). "To set one's face" is a Semitic expression that communicates an unrelenting and steely resolve to accomplish a mission in a way that brooks no opposition and tolerates no delay. "Jerusalem" represents the place where he would bring his life's work to culmination through his passion and death. It was in Jerusalem that Jesus clearly subverted the established order by driving the moneychangers from the temple. Jesus stood his ground firmly and held on unwaveringly to his convictions. Having his own motives for pursuing his course of action, Jesus was not a tragic hero whose life was snatched from him by forces beyond his control. Rather, he asserted, "I lay down my life in order to take it up again. No one takes it from me, but I lay it down of my own accord. I have power to lay it down, and I have power to take it up again. I have received this command from my Father" (John 10:17–18). Here, Jesus was not being "macho," but rather was using his masculine energy to carry out his mission.

Balancing Jesus' masculine energy was his capacity for patient endurance, his comfort with bodily touch, and his openness to intimate relationships—human qualities associated with the *anima*. In spite of the aggression of those who opposed him, Jesus patiently endured hardship with the gentleness and compassion of the Suffering Servant of the Old Testament (see Matt 12:18–21). Like the paschal lamb presented in Isaiah's fourth Servant Song (53:7), Jesus chose a nonviolent stance, even when being tortured and put to death. Furthermore, his connection to his feminine side enabled him to be comfortable with his body and with being touched, as can be seen in his encounter with the penitent woman who anointed his feet with her tears and dried them with her hair, all the while covering them with kisses (see Luke 7:36–50). Possessing a peaceful acceptance of his embodiment as a person, Jesus was at ease with a woman who showed her feelings in such sensuous ways. He was not put off by her reputation as someone with "a bad name in town" and was comfortable with letting her come close and shed her tears of sorrow. By allowing her to show her love in the way that she knew how, Jesus respected her integrity and enabled her to feel whole and good about herself.

Finally, Jesus' feminine energy was clearly manifested in his capacity for affectionate relationships. When observers at the tomb of Lazarus witnessed Jesus' deep sighs and tears, for example, they commented on the obvious depth of his love for a friend (see John 11:32–35). The scene of the Last Supper, as depicted in John's Gospel, provides a vivid illustration of Jesus' ability for human closeness. Once again, he is shown to be comfortably at ease in allowing John, the disciple whom he loved, to recline next to him (see John 13:23–24). The designation, "the disciple Jesus loved," is meant to be a descriptor of all those who follow Jesus, according to some scriptural scholars. Literally, the text states that the beloved disciple rested in Jesus' *kolpos*, the Greek word for "bosom" or "breast." This word is used only twice in John's Gospel: here in the scene of the Last Supper in which Jesus and John, the beloved disciple, are in intimate contact, and in the Prologue of the Gospel, which states that "No one has ever seen God. It is God the only Son, who is close to the Father's heart (*kolpos*), who has made him known" (John 1:18). Relationship, an important feminine value, was essential to Jesus' identity and mission. His relationship with God formed the basis of his self-understanding because his central identity as Son linked him inextricably to God as Father. And Jesus clearly articulated his message in relational terms: "As the Father has loved me, so I have loved you; abide in my love....This is my commandment, that you love one another as I have loved you" (John 15:9, 12).

JESUS' CENTRAL CONCERN: TO EMPOWER THE IMAGINATION

Despite their persistent clamor for cures and miracles, Jesus knew intuitively that what the desperate people who came to him needed was love, more than miraculous cures. Thus, he encouraged them to imagine God as someone who loved them dearly. The intimate relationship that he shared with God as Abba was meant for all to share. To the religious establishment, Jesus' claim to such familiarity with God was tantamount to blasphemy. And his persistence in encouraging his listeners to imagine such intimacy with the Holy One angered the officials responsible for maintaining religious observance. Yet, Jesus stayed on message throughout his ministry and challenged people to imagine a loving God, who was caring and approachable. His listeners needed strong encouragement because they were accustomed to the many religious restrictions placed on God's generous love. They labored under the false assumption that being a foreigner, a tax collector, a woman, or a sinner put them on the wrong side of God—an assumption reinforced by their religious authorities. Yet, Jesus was determined to liberate their imaginations so that they could imagine a God whose love embraces everyone equally, and causes the sun to shine on the good and the bad, the rain to fall on the just and the unjust (see Matt 5:45). Jesus encouraged them to imagine a God of abundant care and generosity. And knowing the longing of the human heart for comfort in the midst of pain, he showed them by his presence the maternal side of God who shares our suffering and weeps with us.

As we noted in the previous chapter, Jesus frequently used parables to pique the imagination of his listeners, hoping to upend their religious mindset of a strict, rule-oriented God. For example, it was jarring for them to hear the parable of the laborers who worked for a single hour getting paid the same amount as those who worked all day (see Matt 20:1–16). Through this parable of the vineyard workers, Jesus was saying that God's gracious generosity always outstrips all our norms of human fairness. Likewise, the three parables recounted in Luke 15 (about the lost sheep, the lost coin, and the lost son) challenged the mind and imagination to discover anew what God is like. Jesus likened God to a shepherd who leaves his entire flock in search of a missing sheep, when common sense would dictate that he cut his losses and safeguard the remaining sheep. This, said Jesus, is how God responds to those who are spiritually lost. To further stretch their religious imaginations, Jesus invited his listeners to imagine God as a woman who loses a favorite coin and searches high and low for it, then throws a party when she finds it. In this parable, Jesus not only offered his listeners a new image of God, but also a new image of themselves as the lost coin—precious in God's eyes. Finally, in the parable of the prodigal son, Jesus told his listeners that God is like a father who throws a lavish party to celebrate the return of a wayward son who had foolishly squandered his inheritance. Through these parables, Jesus taught people to imagine a God who loved them unconditionally—so unlike the god that they had fashioned out of their negative projections and impoverished imaginations.

Jesus' ministry went beyond providing an empathic presence to those who suffered. He sought to empower the powerless, those who had become apathetic and resigned to the oppression and discrimination that constricted their lives. He did this by helping them to imagine how things could be different.

"*The principal concern of Jesus*," notes theologian Monica Hellwig, "*was to refocus and re-educate their imagination.*" The pervasive and "crippling fear of a generally oppressed consciousness" seemed to have withered their power to image God or their own future or the possibilities of their own present society. "*And this paralysis of imagination was evidently projected onto God as the harsh judge and taskmaster, as the distant one*"[9] (emphasis added).

As in Jesus' time, much of the inner suffering that people struggle with today is abetted by an impoverished religious imagination that is unable to envision a God of unfailing love—a love that embraces all of us unconditionally, just as we are. Instead, our projections of a harsh and demanding God leave us with feelings of shame and a sense that we have disappointed God. Many of us are burdened by a strict conscience that demands perfection, thinking this is what God wants. We have an image of holiness that is out of reach for the simple reason that perfection is beyond our grasp. When we inevitably fail, we feel guilty and ashamed and are confirmed in our belief that we are unworthy of God's love. Reflecting on his experience with gang members or "homies" in East Los Angeles, Jesuit priest Greg Boyle states, "Homies seem to live in the zip code of the eternally disappointing, and need a change of address. To this end, one hopes (against all human inclination) to model not the 'one false move' God but the 'no matter whatness' of God. You seek to imitate the kind of God you believe in, where disappointment is, well, Greek to Him. You strive to live the black spiritual that says, 'God looks beyond our fault and sees our need.'"[10]

Based on our belief that the healing of shame is rooted in a return to the feminine, we want to highlight the maternal nature of God's love as it is manifested in the person of Jesus. The Letter to the Hebrews proclaims that in Jesus, we have a compassionate high priest, "who in every respect has been tested as we are, yet without sin" (4:15–16). Truly human like us, Jesus "is able to deal gently with the ignorant and wayward, since he himself is subject to weakness" (5:2). Reflecting on the meaning of the incarnation, Anne Lamott is theologically sound in her graphic depiction of Jesus' human development. Like all of us, he "had to learn by doing, by failing, by feeling, by being amazed."

> God sent Jesus to join the human experience, which means to make a lot of mistakes. Jesus didn't arrive here knowing how to walk. He had fingers and toes, confusion, sexual feelings, crazy human internal processes. He had the same prejudices as the rest of his tribe: he had to learn that the Canaanite woman was a person. He had to suffer the hardships and tedium and setbacks of being a regular person. If he hadn't, the Incarnation would mean nothing.[11]

Thus, scripture encourages us to "approach the throne of grace with boldness, so that we may receive mercy and find grace to help in time of need" (Heb 4:16).

This emphasis on a return to the feminine is supported by Jungian analyst Marion Woodman, who believes that perfectionism stems from a cultural overemphasis on the masculine principle and a suppression of the feminine. "Essentially I am suggesting," states Woodman, "that many of us—men and women—are addicted in one way or another because our patriarchal culture emphasizes specialization and perfection. Driven to do our best at school, on the job, in our relationships—in every corner of our lives—we try to make ourselves into works of art. Working so hard to create our own perfection we forget that we are human beings."[12] She relates perfectionism to the domination of masculine consciousness. Symbolized by the head, the masculine principle (*animus*) values order, power, and perfection, while the feminine (*anima*), symbolized by the heart, cherishes feelings, relationships, and mystery.

THE HUMAN EXPERIENCE OF JESUS

Suffering—our own and that of others—can soften our hearts and school us in compassion. This is true for us, as it was for Jesus. How might we understand this aspect of Jesus' life? As a literary genre, gospel literature is distinct from works of history. Gospels are meant to convey religious testimony, not historical facts. Thus, the Gospels don't provide us with biographical information, chronicling how Jesus experienced personal struggles and suffering, though the passion accounts do give us a graphic description of the painful ordeal of his final days. To truly understand how Jesus' compassion was shaped by his life experiences, we need to imagine how he might have struggled with aspects of life that humans generally find difficult. When we read between the lines, with the help of our imaginations, we can intuit from the Gospels some of the emotional struggles of the human Jesus.

For example, how might Jesus have experienced shame? We know that we feel deep shame when people we know reject us. This was clearly the experience of Jesus, who "came to what was his own, and his own people did not accept him" (John 1:11). He must have felt rejected when close friends turned their backs on him—Judas's betraying him with a kiss and Peter's denying his friendship before a crowd gathered in front of the high priest's residence. But even closer to home, we can imagine that Jesus felt misunderstood by his own family. Early in his public ministry, such crowds gathered around Jesus that he "could not even eat. When his family heard it, they went out to restrain him, for people were saying, 'He has gone out of his mind.'" (Mark 3:20–21). This event bears some similarity to what today is called a "family intervention" when someone is seen as troubled and out of control. It is not a stretch to think that this was a shameful personal experience for Jesus. Later, we read that when Jesus returned to his home in Nazareth for a visit, he was greeted with cold suspicion: "'Is not this the carpenter, the son of Mary and brother of James and Joses and Judas and Simon, and are not his sisters here with us?' And they took offense at him." Jesus was so affected by their lack of faith in him that he could work no miracles there (see Mark 6:3–6). After incurring such animosity and opposition even from his relatives and former neighbors, Jesus observed that "foxes have holes, and birds of the air have nests; but the Son of Man has nowhere to lay his head" (Luke 9:58).

Being a disappointment to many must also have caused Jesus pain and frustration. He knew that he disappointed people who had expectations of him that did not match his own sense of vocation. Those who sought a political messiah to lead a violent overthrow of the Roman occupiers were disillusioned by Jesus' message of universal love and nonviolent resistance. Others, like those who pursued Jesus after the miracle of the multiplication of the loaves, fixed their narrow focus on the tangible benefits that Jesus could provide. Even some of his disciples, like the two disenchanted followers returning home to Emmaus after witnessing Jesus' disgraceful death in Jerusalem, found it hard to disguise their disappointment. Clearly, they felt let down. It is not hard to imagine that Jesus would have felt drained by the resistance he encountered and the discontent that he saw in the faces of the many people who walked away from him.

Jesus faced a daunting task in trying to reconcile the existence of a God of love with the reality of human suffering. People who experience the harshness of life—be it poverty, illness, abuse, or powerlessness—often think that God is punishing or testing them, or that God doesn't hear their prayers, or even that there is no God. Such was the plight of many who gravitated to Jesus, looking for hope and relief. Endo sensitively imagines how this might have affected Jesus:

> He [Jesus] had faith in the love of God. He was so moved by this love that wherever he saw the pitiable men and women of Galilee, he wanted to share their suffering. He could not think, since God was Love itself, that God would forsake these people. Yet no one could appreciate the mystery of God's love. The people by the Lake of Galilee eventually fell away from Jesus because they demanded material benefits rather than love, and so Jesus prayed earnestly to God for guidance to discern what best to do in this situation.[13]

Another source of pain for Jesus could have been the rumors spread by detractors who "began to move around and to pass the word that Jesus was a 'bastard' (Hebrew: *mamzer*) and a 'wine-bibber and a glutton'—anything to tear down the public opinion which favored him."[14] In the middle of a heated debate with those who sought to discredit him, Jesus felt the shaming accusations of his opponents. Jesus said to them, "'You are trying to kill me, a man who has told you the truth that I heard from God'....They said to him, '*We* are not illegitimate children; we have one father, God himself'" (John 8:40–41, emphasis added). The emphasis that "*We* are not illegitimate" carries the malicious implication that Jesus was. In response, Jesus stood his ground: "If God were your Father, you would love me, for I came from God and now I am here. I did not come on my own, but he sent me. Why do you not understand what I say?" (John 8:42–43). Imagine how hurt and rejected Jesus must have felt by being so misunderstood and maligned. Given these assaults on his character, we can appreciate Stephen Mitchell's depiction of Jesus' baptism in the Jordan and why it had such a profound impact on him:

> As Jesus looked into his [John the Baptist's] eyes or as he was thrust under the surface of the Jordan River,

something broke open, not in the heavens but in his own heart. He felt an ecstatic release, a cleansing of those painful hidden childhood emotions of humiliation and shame, a sense of being taken up, once and for all, into the embrace of God. "You are my beloved son; this day I have begotten you."[15]

Jesus' polemic with the Jewish leaders who violently resisted his claim to religious authority is dramatically described in the account in John's Gospel when "the Jews took up stones again to stone him" (10:31). Exasperated by their stubborn refusal to believe in him, Jesus finally pleads with them to judge him by his actions, if they will not accept his word. "If I am not doing the works of my Father, then do not believe me. But if I do them, even though you do not believe me, believe the works" (10:37–38). The plea of Jesus fell on deaf ears, as "they tried to arrest him again, but he escaped from their hands" (10:39). Physically and psychologically shaken by this outright rejection, Jesus returns to the other side of the Jordan, "where John had been baptizing earlier, and he remained there" (10:40). The significance of the three verses that serve as a literary transition from chapter 10 to chapter 11 can be easily overlooked. Yet, they contain key insights into Jesus' spiritual life. Notice that after a bruising encounter with his foes, a battered Jesus returns to the site of his baptism. He not only revisits the place, but *remains* there. The Greek word used here for "to stay" or "to remain" is *menein*, the word that, in John's usage, conveys closeness and intimacy. It can be argued that Jesus revisited the event of his baptism because it was his foundational religious experience. This text supports what our religious imagination intuits—that whenever Jesus was shaken by hardships in his ministry, he spent the night in prayer in order to savor the grace of his baptism and to be reassured of his *Abba's* ongoing love and support. "You are my Son, the Beloved; with you I am well pleased" (Luke 3:22).

JESUS, THE IMAGE OF
THE INVISIBLE GOD

In Jesus, we have a tangible connection to God's love for us. He tells us, "As the Father has loved me, so I have loved you" (John 15:9). To grow closer to God in intimacy, we need to deepen our appreciation of the incarnation. Early in Luke's Gospel, we hear the core of the good news summed up in Zechariah's exuberant prophecy—that in Jesus, God's "faithful love" and tender mercy would be clearly manifested for the salvation of all (see Luke 1:78). The incarnation reveals the depth of God's love because it shows us that God was not satisfied with loving us from afar, but wanted to be closer to us. In the humanity of Jesus, we can experience palpably God's love. In his *Spiritual Exercises*, Ignatius of Loyola reveals two key insights into the important role Jesus performs in connecting us with God. First, Jesus is the compassion of God made visible for us to see and to experience. Second, the principal activity of the risen Jesus is to be a consoler. Ignatius hoped that in experiencing Jesus, we would encounter the compassion and consolation of God in a profoundly healing and transforming way.

The first insight of Ignatius—that Jesus manifests the compassion of God—is contained in his suggestion about how we might pray over the mystery of the incarnation.[16] Ignatius invites us to imagine the three persons of the Trinity hovering over the earth, witnessing the sufferings of humanity—people of diverse races and cultures, of various sizes and life situations, all struggling and seemingly lost. The sight of human suffering moves the three persons of the Trinity with compassion, and they decide that one of them should become human so that this divine compassion could be perceived and felt by humans. So they decide that the second person, the eternal Word, should become human; thus "the Word became flesh and lived among us" (John 1:14)—or, in the poetic language of the Prologue of John's Gospel, the Word "pitched his tent among us" (*eskenosen*). What a wonderful image this is to convey of the nearness of God to John's audience of tent-dwellers in a Bedouin culture. In this imaginative depiction of the

91

incarnation, Ignatius hoped that we would share the joyful experience of the author of the First Letter of John: "We declare to you what was from the beginning, what we have heard, what we have seen with our eyes, what we have looked at and touched with our hands, concerning the word of life—this life was revealed, and we have seen it and testify to it....We are writing these things so that our joy may be complete" (1:1–2, 4). For Ignatius, contemplating the incarnation of Jesus deepens our felt-knowledge of God's love made so real in Jesus' life.

The second key Ignatian insight—that Jesus links us intimately with God's caring presence—is contained in his description of the risen Jesus. In one of his suggestions about how to pray over the resurrection of Jesus, Ignatius invites us to "consider the office of consoler that Christ our Lord exercises, and compare it with the way in which friends are wont to console each other."[17] The resurrection narratives in the Gospels illustrate how the risen Jesus consoles his grief-stricken followers with tenderness and care. Appearing to them, his greeting, "Peace, do not be afraid. It is I," lifted their heavy hearts and enabled them to rejoice. The experiences of Mary at the tomb, of Peter at the shore of Galilee, and of the two disciples returning home from Jerusalem, for example, graphically portray the risen Jesus at work as Consoler. To a heartbroken Mary Magdalene, distressed that she cannot find the body of the one she so loved, the risen Jesus brings consolation. At the sound of Jesus calling her by name, she realizes that Jesus is alive. Peter, filled with guilt and shame after his triple denial of Jesus, encounters the friend he betrayed and feels deeply consoled by being forgiven and reconciled with Jesus, and consoled also by regaining his commission to lead the church, which he had forfeited by his denial. Finally, the risen Jesus brings consolation to two disillusioned disciples on the way home from Jerusalem, where their hopes were dashed by Jesus' death. They experience the risen Jesus when he shares a meal with them and enflames their hearts with new hope. These gospel illustrations are meant to convey to Christian believers that the post-Easter Jesus remains in our midst as an abiding source of divine consolation. In Ignatian spirituality, spiritual consolation is a felt experience of peace and joy and a reliable indication of the near presence of God. Through experiences of consolation, we come to a realization of God's active presence in our lives.

DISCIPLESHIP: A CALL TO EMBODY THE COMPASSION OF JESUS

Whatever form our lives take, we are called as Christians to give flesh-and-blood reality to the ongoing compassion of God for all. That is how Jesuit priest Greg Boyle understands the nature of his work with gang members. "God is compassionate, loving kindness," he writes. "All we're asked to do is to be in the world who God is. Certainly compassion was the wallpaper of Jesus' soul, the contour of his heart, it was who he was."[18] That God depends on us to embody the love of Jesus for others is the message in the following story: A statue of Jesus wrecked by the shelling during World War II stood just outside a small village near Normandy. Its hands had been totally destroyed. After the war, the villagers gathered around the ruined statue to decide its fate. One group argued that the statue was so badly damaged that it should be trashed and a new one erected in its place. Another group objected, arguing that the village artisan whose specialty was the restoration of damaged art objects could easily take care of the job. Finally, a third group voiced a proposal that ultimately carried the day: that the statue be cleaned up, but remain handless; and that a plaque be placed at its base with the inscription: "I have no hands but yours."

Sr. Helen Prejean's ministry to those on death row powerfully illustrates what it means to "give God a face that others can see." In her best-selling book, *Dead Man Walking*, she recounts her experience with Patrick Sonnier, who was convicted of murder and faced the death penalty. In one of her many visits with him, she comforted him, saying, "I can't bear the thought that you would die without seeing one loving face. I will be the face of Christ for you."[19] Just as Jesus was the image of a caring, albeit invisible, God

93

for those afflicted by pain and suffering, Sr. Helen gives the risen Jesus a face that others can see and, in this way, enables people to experience the abiding love and compassion of God today.

Similarly, the story of a young man killed in a drive-by shooting illustrates the call we all share to stand in place of Jesus for those who cry out for love and reassurance. The wounded man lay dying in front of the church as a group of horrified parishioners gathered around him, waiting for the paramedics to arrive. As his life energies steadily slipped away, the young man could be heard over and over again crying out for his mother, seemingly to no avail. Suddenly, a woman broke through the crowd and bent down to cradle the dying man in her arms. Gently rocking him, she repeated in soothing and reassuring tones, "I'm here, son. Everything's going to be okay." As the dying man breathed his last breath, she blessed him with the sign of the cross. A few days later, the woman, filled with scruples, appeared at the door of the rectory. She wanted to confess that she had lied, that she was not really the mother of the young man who had died. She felt guilty for what she had done, even though at the time she felt drawn to do whatever was needed to comfort the dying man crying out for his mother. She left the rectory with peace of mind and a sense of validation, because the priest had reassured her that she not only had done nothing wrong, but, in fact, had responded in a most Christlike way. Like Jesus, she had embodied the compassion of God for another. To embody the presence of Jesus is to emulate his sensitivity and care for those in need.

FOLLOWING THE PATH OF THE COMPASSIONATE CHRIST

Embodying the attitudes and values of Jesus lies at the heart of Christian compassion. The Gospel accounts provide an opportunity to witness how Jesus mediated the compassion of God for those in need. Jesus perceived people and events in a way that brought forth compassion. The plight of others always stirred his heart and moved him to reach out in healing and forgiving ways. Once a leper approached Jesus, begging to be cured (see Mark 1:40–45). Jesus took in the reality of this afflicted suppliant, paying close attention to his words and actions. Then, moved with compassion, he reached out to touch the diseased person. Jesus' therapeutic touch issued forth from a compassionate heart. This episode exemplifies a threefold dynamic that characterizes many of Jesus' ministerial encounters: first, Jesus is keenly aware of his interpersonal environment, sensitive to the needs of the people around him; second, he lets what he perceives stir him to compassion; and third, moved by compassion, he reaches out to help.

"Perceiving" or "seeing" can be said to be the beginning of all compassionate action. Clearly, this was the case with Jesus. To imitate the loving actions of Jesus is to perceive people and events compassionately. A story told by Bishop Gerald Barnes of San Bernardino, California, illustrates the power of perception to influence feelings and behavior. In an address to a national conference, the bishop gave a brief account of his background. Having spent part of his childhood in the projects of East Los Angeles, he and his family were familiar with poverty. After many years of struggle, his father was able to buy a mom-and-pop grocery store above which the family made its home. He went on to recall an incident that occurred when he was a seminarian, riding in the back of his parents' car. As the automobile made its way through skid row in Los Angeles, Barnes's father had to slam on the brakes just before a traffic light to avoid hitting a man who was running across the street. Bishop Barnes recounted the pointed conversation that then took place between him and his mother:

> I said, "Look at that bum. What a waste." My mother turned around and looked right at me in the back seat and said, "He has a mother. He's someone's son." "I saw a bum. She saw someone's son," he told the audience in his keynote speech.

Barnes contrasted his own haughty attitude with his mother's grace: "I was a seminarian. I was studying scripture. Attending daily Mass, I saw a nobody. She was living the Scriptures. She saw with faith. I was the righteous, arrogant kid. She was compassionate. She saw kinship. A different view. I looked at him with disdain. She looked at him with acceptance. He was somebody."[20]

Jesus' caring outreach to the leper, who was ostracized from society on account of his ailment, was typical of Jesus. Other outcasts of his day—women, foreigners, tax collectors, and prostitutes—all received compassion from Jesus, even as their religious leaders denied them access to the official channels of healing and reconciliation. In addition to the care he showed toward individuals, Jesus' compassion also extended to groups. In its two accounts of the miracles of the multiplication of the loaves and fishes, Mark's Gospel illustrates Jesus' sensitive perception and compassionate response toward the needs of the masses. In one account (see Mark 8:1–10), Jesus is moved to action as he becomes aware of the crowd's hunger. Realizing that those who had gathered to hear his words were without food, Jesus expressed his concern: "I have compassion for the crowd, because they have been with me now for three days and have nothing to eat. If I send them away hungry to their homes, they will faint on the way—and some of them have come from a great distance" (8:2–3).

In contrast, in the other account (see Mark 6:30–44), Jesus perceived a different need that, nonetheless, elicited the same compassionate response. Here, Jesus is said to have acted because he saw in the crowd, not a physical hunger for food, but a spiritual hunger for guidance and meaning. Jesus "had compassion for them, because they were like sheep without a shepherd; and he began to teach them many things" (6:34). While each account attributes a different reason for Jesus' compassionate response to the crowd, they both point unambiguously to the same sensitive quality of Jesus' perception of others and events. In both accounts, Jesus' ministerial outreach begins with a perception of others that is sufficiently sensitive to arouse feelings of compassionate concern.

These stories of Jesus' interactions with individuals and groups reveal his keen sensitivity to those around him and his broad understanding of their needs as human beings. The miracles of the multiplication of the loaves and fishes dramatize the reality of the incarnation—God's love, embodied in the person of Jesus Christ, flows from an empathic understanding of and solidarity with all humankind.

SPIRITUAL EXERCISES AND REFLECTION

A. The Caring Approach of God Comes Mainly through People

As Jesuit poet Gerard Manley Hopkins expresses so elo-quently:

> —for Christ plays in ten thousand places,
> Lovely in limbs, and lovely in eyes not his
> To the Father through the features of men's faces.[21]

Just as Sr. Helen Prejean was "the face of Christ" for a person facing the death penalty, people have similarly enabled each of us to experience the care and compassion of the risen Jesus through their presence and actions in our lives.

> Who comes to mind when you reflect on those who have embodied the risen Jesus' presence and love for you? Relive a time when you experienced such love. What in the other person's presence and behavior touched you so lovingly? Say a prayer of gratitude for that person.
> Who comes to mind when you reflect on those in your life who need you to be present in such a way that they can see the face of Christ in you? What are you

moved to do or say in order to reach out to them in a compassionate way?

B. Extending a Healing Touch through an Imaginative Prayer

1. Bring to mind someone in your life who is currently suffering in some way—physically, emotionally, or mentally.
2. Using your imagination, try to get a concrete sense of what this person is going through: Where in his or her body might he or she be experiencing pain? What painful feelings might he or she be having?
3. Think of a metaphor or image that would capture this person's struggle. For example: "Feeling his age, he's afraid of being shelved and ignored." "She feels bone-tired and stretched to the breaking point, trying to take care of her kids and her aging parents at the same time." "The pain in his feet makes him feel like he's walking on hot rocks." "She constantly stammers when expressing her opinion, like someone facing a judge and jury."
4. Imagine that you are with the suffering person and that your presence—the way you look, listen, and speak—makes him or her feel loved and supported. See how consoled and healed he or she feels by your words and actions.
5. If you imagine yourself in this person's place, what grace would you most desire? Then ask God to give the suffering person this grace, as you end your prayer.

CHAPTER FIVE
GOSPEL STORIES OF CONSOLING LOVE

"The joy of the Gospel fills the hearts and lives of all who encounter Jesus….With Christ joy is constantly born anew."
—Pope Francis, *The Joy of the Gospel* (no. 1)

A Chinese proverb states, "One picture is worth a thousand words." The same can be said of a story. Stories help us to see with the heart and engage us totally—enlightening our minds and stimulating our senses and imaginations. That is why, from ancient times, people have relied heavily on stories to convey important truths. Stories give us access to the drama of human lives by showing rather than telling. They create pictures that open our eyes and spark our feelings, moving us beyond mere understanding. For this reason, we as Christians read biblical stories over and over "until we finally start seeing the same story of healing and hope in the twists and turns of our own stories of life with God."[1] When we truly realize that God is with us in all our ups and downs, our joys and sorrows, we know we are not alone.

In this chapter, we reimagine some familiar Gospel stories that illustrate Jesus' compassion and care for those who came to him in need. While these stories are known to most Christians, they take on deeper meaning when viewed as stories that express Jesus' deep desire to heal those burdened by guilt and shame. What touches us and draws us into these stories is the way they picture Jesus spending his time with people who were ignored or rejected by others.

99

Praying with these stories helps us to realize that no matter how undeserving we may feel, God is paying attention to us and is present to us in our struggles. Gospel stories contain "good news" because they illustrate not only what God did in the past, but also what God is always doing. Retelling stories of Jesus' compassionate ministry encourages a more intimate way of praying, as we become part of the story. Scriptural prayer is most fruitful when "we live inside the stories of Jesus and bring our contemporary experiences to them. By imaginatively entering into the stories of Jesus, we can 'hear' what Jesus has to say to us in our situation."[2]

Biblical stories help us to spot the myriad and often mysterious ways in which God intervenes when we most need help. For example:

- The story of Jesus' cure of the man at the pool of Bethesda (see John 5:1–9) reveals a God who intervenes to liberate people who are paralyzed by fear and unable to help themselves.
- The story of the death and resurrection of Jesus reveals the action of a God who promises to bring new life wherever we experience death and diminishment.
- The story of the frightful crossing of the tempestuous Lake of Galilee by the timid disciples (see Mark 4:35–41; Matt 8:18, 23–27; Luke 8:22–25) reveals a God who is present in the stormy transitions of our lives, assuring us that we need not be afraid.
- The story of Mary's annunciation (see Luke 1:26–38) reveals a God who may break into the routine of our lives in annunciation-like moments to summon us into an unknown, yet hopeful, future.

When we recognize the similarity between a scriptural event and one of our present situations, it is as if scales drop from our eyes and we recognize the divine presence in an "aha" moment. Then, like

Moses before the burning bush, we can only cover our faces and stand in awe of God (see Exod 3:6).

CONNECTING WITH THE JOY OF THE GOSPEL

The word *gospel* literally means "good news." As Pope Francis states in his first pastoral letter, the "joy of the Gospel" should fill "the hearts and lives of all who encounter Jesus." Why, then, for so many people, is the gospel neither "good" nor "news"? It can't be that people no longer need the good news, or that people no longer seek God. While many things might contribute to this situation, two immediately come to mind: fundamentalism and familiarity. Fundamentalism entails a literal, one-dimensional reading of the Bible, without appreciation for its symbolic language and rich metaphors. Metaphors go beyond mere description and evoke an affective appreciation of truth. To say, for example, "A mighty fortress is our God" or "God is the rock of our salvation" stirs the heart with trust and confidence. In contrast, to say "God is all powerful" is literally true, but does not echo in our soul as reassuring good news. When Gospel stories are read as if they were mere descriptive reports of events, they fail to capture the emotions and intensity of the events. We can uncover the richness of Gospel stories by appreciating anew their images and metaphors. Metaphors function as a bridge between past biblical events and our present lives, because they "are enormously elastic to touch all kinds of experiences. For example, the dead daughter of Jairus can be the child within ourselves that has died; the adultery forgiven by Jesus can be our own forms of infidelity being forgiven; the road to Emmaus becomes our own journey from despair to hope; Jesus' saying not to worry about food and clothes can speak to us about all that disturbs our lives."[3] By making colorful stories monochromatic, fundamentalism deadens the living word of God and deafens us to the good news that these stories proclaim.

We all know what happens when something becomes familiar—we take it for granted. Familiarity also makes us take the Gospels for granted, so that they become "old news." Familiarity lures us into thinking that there is nothing new for us in these stories that we have heard from childhood. We pay halfhearted attention, because we think we already know how they end and what they mean. Consider, for example, the story of the three wise men from the east who find the infant Jesus in a manger in Bethlehem (see Matt 2:1–12). This story is retold every Christmas. Taken as a literal description of a past event, it seems to have no relevance to us today. Yet, taken symbolically, its deeper message is revealed. The images and metaphors of this story tell us that God is more present to us than we often imagine! Familiarity makes us think that the message is simple and one-dimensional: the three kings finally discover the Messiah only at the end of their long search. But the story is so much richer. The three wise men experienced God's presence in at least four other ways: in the stirring in their hearts that launched their search in the first place; in their companionship on cold and lonely nights far from home; in a star that kept them on track; and in a dream that warned them to avoid Herod on their return home. God was with them not only at the end, but all along the way. Familiarity can obscure this story's glad tidings of joy: God's loving presence not only awaits us at the end of our earthly journey, but also accompanies us in myriad ways throughout our lives.

To counteract the dulling effect that fundamentalism and familiarity can have on the good news of the gospel, we want to suggest how the imagination can bring new relevance and fresh appreciation to Gospel stories. The remainder of the chapter is devoted to examples of what an imaginative retelling of biblical stories might look like. Our goal in doing this is to

- deepen the reader's appreciation for Gospel stories as rich repositories of the good news proclaimed by Jesus, and

- show that Gospel stories, when prayed over with imaginative eyes and open hearts, can help us recognize God's healing presence in our lives.

To get the most out of these stories, we suggest using each story as a topic for meditation at different times of prayer. The following reflection questions are meant to deepen your experience:

1. When reading over the Gospel story, pay attention to how you are moved. What feelings are evoked in you?
2. Which characters do you most identify with and feel most attracted to? Which characters do you least identify with and have negative feelings toward?
3. What concerns or issues in your life are reflected in the story?
4. Are you drawn to spend more time with this particular story? In praying with this story, what grace would you like to receive? What desire of your heart do you want God to satisfy?

Jesus and the Bent-Over Woman (*Luke 13:10–13*)

The Gospels portray Jesus as one whose care extended to strangers and friends alike. His compassionate outreach was sometimes a response to a request. At other times, he just noticed people suffering and was moved to alleviate their pain. One Sabbath, for example, while teaching in the synagogue, his eyes happened to spot a woman who was terribly deformed, bent over double. Oppressed by a crippling spirit for eighteen years, she was unable to stand upright. Noticing her painful condition, Jesus called her over and said to her, "Woman, you are freed from your disability," and laid his hands on her. Right away, she straightened up, glorifying God.

This woman symbolizes all of us, both men and women, when we feel unable to stand tall and face life head-on. Some of us are crippled by shame, the dreadful feeling that we are defective and unworthy of love. Some are handicapped by emotional wounds from childhood. And some are diminished by the oppression of prejudice and discrimination, and unjustly denied equal access to educational and work opportunities. The burdens of life can at times be so heavy that it is not difficult to identify with this bent-over woman.

Jesus' awareness of this crippled woman's hardship and his care for her is a story of consolation. Made whole by Jesus, she becomes a symbol of hope, reminding us that the risen Jesus responds to our suffering in the same compassionate way. Her story inspires us to have faith in the healing power of Christ that comes to us in graceful and often unexpected ways, frequently, as noted in the previous chapter, through the approach of people. Believing that God will be there for us may not come easily if our capacity to trust was damaged early in life. If we were neglected or abused in some way, we learned to rely on ourselves. Contemplating stories such as this one can help us to overcome our reluctance to rely on God. When we let go of trying to be self-sufficient, we allow God to enter more intimately into our lives.

Jesus Honors the Short Tax Collector
(*Luke 19:1–10*)

The healing of shame begins when we are accepted for who we are. This was the experience of Zacchaeus, a senior tax collector and a wealthy man, in his encounter with Jesus. His years of hard work had paid off handsomely and landed him a top position in a secure profession. His only problem was that his neighbors and friends despised him for doing the dirty work of collecting taxes for the foreign occupiers of their land. Seen as a sellout, he was reviled and socially scorned. On top of that, he felt self-conscious and embarrassed about his height, ashamed that he was so short.

Well into midlife, he couldn't shake the mild feelings of depression that were always there. Despite having a "good" job and financial security, he felt restless and discontented. So when he read in the *Jerusalem Times* that Jesus of Nazareth, the itinerant preacher who was rumored to be a wise teacher, was going to be passing nearby at noon the next day, he wanted to get a look at him. If what he heard was true, even a glimpse of this holy man might bring him some inner peace and healing. Motivated by this thought, he hatched a plan. He knew he was too short to see above the crowd that would surely gather, but he also knew that there was a sycamore tree along the route that could provide a perch high enough to give him a clear view of Jesus as he walked by. And so, after a restless sleep, he got up early and with great anticipation climbed the sycamore tree and waited.

When Jesus finally reached the spot, Zacchaeus got the surprise of his life. Jesus looked straight up, saw him dangling on a branch, and shouted to him, "Zacchaeus, come down. Hurry because I am to stay at your house today." Startled, Zacchaeus wondered what was happening. All he had hoped for was a tree-limb glance, and now he was being summoned to a face-to-face encounter. And how did Jesus know his name? Beforehand, Zacchaeus felt some comfort in knowing that he would be hidden by the branches and would be anonymous. Not only was Jesus now calling him by name, he was also inviting himself to dinner! Though in a daze, he hurried down and welcomed Jesus with joy. The crowd was also confused by what was happening and began to complain that Jesus was actually going to stay at a sinner's house. But Zacchaeus stood his ground and said to Jesus, "Look, half of my possessions, Lord, I will give to the poor; and if I have defrauded anyone of anything, I will pay back four times as much." Jesus looked lovingly into Zacchaeus's earnest face and acknowledged his goodness and generosity. "Today salvation has come to this house," Jesus reassured him. And in that moment, Zacchaeus felt an overwhelming sense of being accepted. Like a soothing balm, Jesus' love slowly worked its way into his heart and dismantled the shameful stigma of his profession and size.

Jesus and the Samaritan Woman Stuck in Shame (John 4:1–42)

The story of Jesus' encounter with the Samaritan woman at the well highlights a central tenet of Christian faith—that God will meet us just where we are in life and give us what we need to move beyond our past mistakes and failures into a hopeful future.

The woman found herself back at Jacob's well to draw water, as she had done for years. But, after her encounter with Jesus the day before, being at the well was a totally different experience. Now, instead of being alone, she was surrounded by other women from the village, who eagerly pressed her for more details about her conversation with Jesus. They nudged her to share her feelings and impressions of this Jesus whom they too had come to embrace as the long-awaited Messiah. She relished being the center of attention after so many long years of self-imposed isolation, when she would come to the well at the heat of the day, knowing that nobody else would be there. While a part of her yearned for some warm connection with other women in the village, she was afraid and desperate to keep secret her present living situation. Shame and embarrassment welled up in her as she thought about living with a man to whom she was not married. After five failed marriages, she was caught between the fear of yet another unhappy marriage and the desolate prospect of living the rest of her life alone. So she had resigned herself to the present arrangement of just living together with her partner, at least for the time being. But the thought of nosy neighbors probing into her personal life was too much to bear, and so she decided just to stay away from people. Now, however, she was enjoying her newfound friends. She also delighted in the cool morning breeze, which made the chore of drawing water much easier, and thought what a relief it was to no longer have to sneak to the well at noon!

In response to the village women's curiosity about Jesus, she was more than happy to share her impressions. After all, her encounter with him turned out to be the best thing that had ever happened to her.

When I first saw him approaching the well, my instinct was to make a fast getaway. You know how badly we're treated by men and by Jews in general, and I wasn't in any mood to set myself up for grief. It's a real pain that as Samaritans and as women, we're doubly vulnerable to prejudice. Anyway, before I could get my stuff together and dash off, he was right in my face, asking me for a drink. Impulsively, I tried to push him away with an abrupt and unfriendly response: "What? You are a Jew and you're asking me, a Samaritan, for a drink? What's up? Usually, you barely acknowledge our existence!"

But his gentle and respectful response took me by surprise. Then I noticed the tenderness in his eyes and the warmth in his voice. I could feel my resistance softening. Then, I don't quite know how, but one thing led to another, and before I knew it, I had blurted out my whole life story. But to my surprise, instead of feeling exposed and raw, I felt understood and accepted. I think his patient and nonjudgmental manner of listening melted my defenses and allowed me to feel his care!

Never before have I experienced such compassion and sensitivity. Right away, I could tell that Jesus sensed my awkwardness in talking with him. I noticed how he tried to reassure me by approaching gently, in a non-threatening way, with a request: "May I have a drink?" Then, from his look and responses, I could sense that he really was attuned to the deep pain that still lingers from my five unsuccessful marriages. His eyes read my constant struggle not to give in to self-rejection and shame. He knew how rough life has been for me. Then, when I told him about how tired I was and how I wanted some relief from the daily drudgery of coming to the well for water, he taught me about "living water" that would allow me never to thirst again. In talking to Jesus, I felt like I was talking to a very close friend who could intuit behind my words my underlying concerns and feelings. In the end, that's what opened my heart to receiving the revelation of God and made a believer of me.

Jesus Hears the Whole Truth from the Woman with Internal Bleeding (*Mark 5:25–34*)

Sometimes chronic illness can cause shame, especially when we sense that others feel inconvenienced by our condition or don't really understand why we feel so bad, because our symptoms are not noticeable. At times, we can feel judged for not doing more to get well. The story of a woman with a long-term illness and her healing encounter with Jesus can console us when we feel alone with our illnesses and have lost hope that we might be healed.

Mark's Gospel recounts the story of a woman who was cured of chronic internal bleeding by touching the hem of Jesus' cloak as he was rushing to the house of a synagogue official whose daughter was desperately ill. When Jesus persisted in asking who had touched him, the woman "fell down before him, and told him the whole truth" (5:33). She told Jesus how she had suffered for twelve years and had spent all her money for long and painful treatments under various doctors without getting better. In fact, she was getting worse. In her desperation, she thought that if she could only touch Jesus' clothes, she would be healed. What is remarkable about this story is that this woman, contrary to the norm of the day, spoke to a man in public. And what is even more astounding is that she shared with a stranger her woman's problem of internal bleeding, something extremely personal! And this intimate sharing was done out in the open, surrounded by a noisy crowd.

Those of us who may be fearful or hesitant to approach Jesus can be encouraged by the tender response of Jesus to this woman's urgent call for help. Imagine what this desperate woman must have seen in the face of Jesus that emboldened her to lay out her problems so honestly and to tell "the whole truth." Might it have been the caring look she saw in his eyes, as well as the sensitive presence of a Jesus who, even when rushing to save someone who was dying, could listen to her sad story with "the ear of the heart"? To "listen with the ear of the heart," as St. Benedict put it in the prologue of his *Rule*, is to let people tell their stories in their own words and in their own ways—without having to worry about being judged, criticized, or interrupted. When our stories are heard with the ear of the heart, we experience the kind of compassionate love that heals. This is how it was for the woman who was cured of her hemorrhage.

Jesus Restores Joy to a Fallen Peter
(John 21:1–23)

A brief review of the events that led to Peter's surprise encounter with the risen Jesus at the Sea of Tiberias makes clear why this was such a profound, personal experience for him. Just a week earlier, tears of shame and guilt were streaming down his face, as he dashed out of the courtyard of the high priest's house where Jesus was being detained. "How could you have betrayed your friend, Jesus?" asked a harsh inner voice. Just a while ago, the thought of turning his back on Jesus had been unthinkable. His words to Jesus, recently spoken with such bravado, now came back to haunt him: "Lord, I am ready to go with you to prison and to death!" (Luke 22:33).

However, just as Jesus had predicted, he had ended up denying the Lord three times. It had all happened so fast, thought Peter. First, he found himself following cautiously, all the way into the courtyard. Then, as he started getting self-conscious about being recognized as a follower of Jesus, it dawned on him that he himself was in danger. That's when the people started accusing him out loud: "You also were with Jesus, the man from Nazareth" (Mark 14:67). He could feel himself tense up. The more people pressed the issue, the more adamant his denial became. In a matter of minutes, his shrug of denial grew into a full-blown oath, when he started calling down curses on himself and swearing, "I do not know the man!" (Matt 26:74). Even as he recalled the swift sequence of events, the bitter pain of failure knotted his stomach, and he felt weighed down by depression. Peter later realized that the look of Jesus in the courtyard when the Lord turned toward him—a look so full of compassion—is what jarred him into awareness that he had done a terrible thing *and* that Jesus understood and forgave him. When that realization hit him, he wept.

At the Sea of Tiberias, still in the process of sorting out his last days with Jesus and his lingering feelings of sorrow, guilt, and sadness, Peter felt suddenly overwhelmed by a deep sense of Jesus' consoling presence. Gratefully, he experienced again that he had been forgiven, recommissioned, and reunited to the dear friend he had betrayed.

That all four Gospels recount Peter's denial indicates that the early Christians proclaimed, not covered up, their first leader's deficiency. Somehow, they were strengthened, not scandalized, by it. Peter's experience reaffirmed for them that sin is forgivable. Very likely, Peter himself had spread the story of his failure, as he tirelessly tried to support the brothers and sisters in their trials as Jesus had asked him to do. "Simon, Simon, listen! Satan has demanded to sift all of you like wheat, but I have prayed for you that your own faith may not fail; and you, when once you have turned back, strengthen your brothers" (Luke 22:31–32). Just as the early Church saw Adam's fall as a "happy fault," because it brought forth a Savior, it also regarded Peter's failing as a *"felix culpa,"* for it produced a compassionate leader. Peter had been forced to face his weakness and had been made humble and compassionate as a result.

"The Look of Jesus," Anthony de Mello's reflection on Peter's painful experience, encourages us to trust always in the steadfast love of Christ:

> I had a fairly good relationship with the Lord. I would ask for things, converse with him, praise him, thank him…
>
> But always I had this uncomfortable feeling that he wanted me to look at him. And I would not. I would talk back, but look away when I sensed he was looking at me.
>
> I was afraid. I should find an accusation there of some unrepented sin. I thought I should find a demand there; there would be something he wanted from me.

One day I finally summoned up courage and looked! There was no accusation. There was no demand. The eyes just said, "I love you."

And I walked out and, like Peter, I wept.[4]

Jesus Affirms the Adulterous Woman
(John 8:3–11)

Jesus' response to the woman caught in adultery shows how he listened to people in such a way that they felt loved by God. Surrounded by self-righteous condemners ready to stone her to death as required by the Law of Moses, she was publically exposed and shamed. Witnessing the scene of the angry men about to stone the woman, Jesus said nothing until the end. He listened to the Pharisees; their words and their anger with him. He also listened to the silence of the woman and heard her guilt, her fears, and her need to be accepted for who she was, without condemnation or judgment. Although she did not speak to Jesus or ask for help, he "heard" her and said these healing words: "Has no one condemned you?...Neither do I condemn you. Go your way, and from now on do not sin again." He didn't feel the need to lecture or admonish her; instead he affirmed her ability to turn her life around. He sent her off, freed from debilitating shame, to rebuild her life.

This Gospel story clearly illustrates an important aspect of the good news proclaimed by Jesus: no matter how low we have been brought by poor choices and shameful mistakes, God always gives us another chance. No wonder some Christian churches are called the Church of Second Chance! But the gospel message extends far beyond just a "second chance" and echoes Jesus' exhortation that we be given "seventy-seven" chances (Matt 18:22). Like the prodigal son, we too live in a multiple-chance universe (see Luke 15:11–32). In the parable of the barren fruit tree (see Luke 13:6–9), a fruitless tree is spared from being cut down and is given yet another year to yield fruit. The recurrent message of Jesus is that an unconditionally loving God always gives us more time to learn from our mistakes and to improve our lives.

Jesus and the Woman Who Loved Much
(*Luke 7:36–50*)

Luke portrays Jesus as a person comfortable with his human-ity and capable of relating deeply with others. In the story of Jesus' intimate encounter with a woman "who had a bad name in the town," we see how he looked beyond negative stereotypes to reach the hurting individual before him. What would have been an awk-ward situation for someone who was uncomfortable with physical contact and the expression of emotion was for Jesus an opportunity to bring healing to someone scorned by others.

Once, when Jesus was dining at a Pharisee's house, a woman barged in bringing with her an alabaster jar of ointment. "She stood behind him at his feet, weeping, and began to bathe his feet with her tears and to dry them with her hair. Then she continued kissing his feet and anointing them with the ointment" (Luke 7:38). At the sight of this, the Pharisee grumbled to himself, "If this man were a prophet, he would have known who and what kind of woman this is who is touching him—that she is a sinner" (7:39).

A way of renewing our appreciation of biblical stories that have been made dull through over-familiarity is to pose a new question to the text. This well-known story has been used tradi-tionally to illustrate the relationship between forgiveness and love: that a person who has been forgiven much, loves much. This is cer-tainly an important insight into the passage. However, a new ques-tion put to this text can uncover another rich message. For example, we might ask, "What can this story teach us about chaste love?"

If we consider the close bodily contact between Jesus and the woman, it reveals a clear example of chaste love. The physical con-tact was highly intimate: the woman anointed Jesus' feet with oil, covered them with kisses, and wiped away her tears with her hair. Although intensely sensual, there was no indication of anything sexually inappropriate in her behavior. Despite her reputation, she showed no hint of being seductive or manipulative. What the Pharisee objected to was not the nature of the contact, but that

Jesus allowed the sinner any contact at all. On the part of Jesus, we see no trace of anything inappropriate—not the slightest indication of someone taking advantage of his power to exploit another for the sake of his own gratification.

This passage shows us why an encounter with Jesus was so healing for those who approached him with their pain. Baring her soul to Jesus in such an intimate way allowed Jesus to mediate God's love for this penitent woman. She was able to be open and emotionally vulnerable because she discovered in Jesus a chaste love that could be trusted. A well-integrated man, Jesus was at ease with a woman who showed her feelings in such sensuous ways. He was comfortable with her touch and her copious tears of sorrow. By allowing her to show her love in the way that she knew how, Jesus respected her integrity and took away her shame. While the Pharisee's disdainful attitude of the woman who had "a bad name in town" was shaming, Jesus' nonjudgmental acceptance was healing.

Jesus Restores Life to the Grieving Widow's Son (*Luke 7:11–17*)

In the story of the raising of the dead son of a widow, Luke powerfully captures Jesus' compassion in action. As the story goes, Jesus and his disciples were approaching the gate of the town of Naim when they encountered a funeral procession and a grieving mother who had just lost her only son. Discovering that she was a widow, who was particularly vulnerable in a patriarchal society without a husband or son to protect her, Jesus felt a surge of compassion for her. He sensed acutely her great loss and suffering. So, without being asked, Jesus reached out to her and said, "'Do not weep.' Then he came forward and touched the bier, and the bearers stood still. And he said, 'Young man, I say to you, rise!' The dead man sat up and began to speak, *and Jesus gave him to his mother*" (Luke 7:13–15; emphasis added).

The original Greek text conveys the intensity and depth of Jesus' reaction to this mother's suffering by using the word

splanchna. This term literally means "entrails" or "inner parts."
Bowels was the symbol for a person's most deep-seated emotion.
The Septuagint—the Greek translation of the Old Testament—
invariably uses this word to designate the mercy of God. It is significant that Luke uses this same term to describe Jesus' reaction to
suffering. In doing so, the Gospel writer is pointing out that Jesus'
compassion reveals the compassion of God. Indeed, Jesus is the
compassion of God.

Lazarus's Story, Our Story Too (*John 11:1–54*)

God will bring new life to us whenever we experience diminishment or death of any kind—this was the centerpiece of Jesus'
message. Christians refer to this mystery of new life coming from
death as the paradox of the paschal mystery. The account of the
raising of Lazarus graphically illustrates this consoling truth of
faith. The contemporary recasting of this ancient story that follows
is meant to help modern ears hear anew the hopeful truth that
undergirds our lives as people who have faith in Jesus, who said, "I
am the resurrection and the life. Those who believe in me, even
though they die, will live, and everyone who lives and believes in
me will never die" (John 11:25–26).

"Miraculous Act Seals Fate of Nazarean," declared the front-
page headlines of the *Jerusalem Times*. The tabloid captured the
attention of Lazarus, his sisters, Mary and Martha, and Jesus, who
had gathered for a private dinner to celebrate Lazarus's miraculous
return to life. They all wondered anxiously how the political fall-
out of this miracle was going to affect them. This is how it was
reported:

> Yesterday, two miles outside of Jerusalem, Jesus of
> Nazareth, an itinerant preacher, is reported to have
> brought back to life a close friend, Lazarus of Bethany,
> who had died of a recent illness and had already been
> buried in a tomb for four days. Details of the dramatic
> event have been supplied by friends who were with
> Lazarus's two sisters when the alleged "resurrection"

occurred, as well as by curious onlookers who rushed to the scene.

Eyewitnesses were many, since the friends who had come to console the deceased's sisters were already gathered at the Bethany home when Jesus, a family friend and frequent dinner guest, arrived. Several days earlier, according to an unidentified source, the sisters had desperately summoned Jesus when Lazarus was close to death. But by the time Jesus arrived, Lazarus had died and was entombed. Testimony from those who witnessed the event agreed that the Nazarean miracle worker seemed to know the sisters personally because he was seen embracing them. According to some observers, Jesus wept, deeply moved by Lazarus's death and his sisters' grief. Watching Jesus weeping, some were overheard saying, "See how much he loved him!"

Once at the tomb, which was a cave with a stone placed at the entrance, the Nazarean ordered the caretakers to remove the stone, even though one of the dead man's sisters warned that there would be a foul smell, since Lazarus had already been buried for four days. When the stone was taken away, Jesus looked up and said, "Thank you, God, for listening to me. I know that you always listen to me, but I say this for the sake of the people here, so that they will believe that you sent me." After saying this, he yelled, "Lazarus, come out!" To the bewilderment of all, the dead man came out, his hands and feet wrapped in burial linen and a cloth around his face. "Untie him," Jesus commanded, "and let him go."

News of the miracle spread quickly throughout Jerusalem and, according to an aide of the High Priest, speaking on the grounds of anonymity, was the single item on the agenda when the Pharisees, High Priest, and the Council met at a hastily convened meeting. The emergency meeting, the aide disclosed, was to determine the Jewish establishment's response to this so-called miracle, which was rapidly attracting huge numbers of followers to Jesus and stirring up dangerous talk about rebellion against the Romans. The fear of those at the meeting was that there would be a repressive clampdown and destruction of the Temple and the Jewish nation by the Roman authorities. While no official report of the proceedings is available, close disciples of Jesus are convinced that plans were made to kill Jesus in order to restore calm to the streets and to reduce the threat of Roman incursion. It is rumored that the chief priests also made plans to kill Lazarus, because on his account, many of the Jews were rejecting them and believing in Jesus, the Nazarean miracle worker.

When they finished reading, Lazarus, Martha, and Mary were filled with mixed emotions—happiness and gratitude to Jesus for bringing Lazarus back to life, but also fear and guilt because Jesus had jeopardized his own life to save Lazarus. When Jesus saw their anguish and concern, he said to them, "Don't let your hearts be troubled, my friends. I'm not surprised by the talk about plots to kill me. Even when I was weeping and trembling before the tomb, I knew the consequences of what I was about to do. But to lay down my life for my friends is the meaning of my life. I know that my life is in danger. But what shall I say? Shall I say, "Father, do not let this hour come upon me?" But this is why I came—to manifest God's great love for all. The hour has come for God to receive great glory through me."

Jesus' words dispelled the tension that had fallen on the group. With relief, Martha rushed to the kitchen to finish up last minute preparations for the meal, while Mary took out a whole pint of very expensive perfume made of pure nard. She poured the perfume on Jesus' feet and lovingly wiped them with her hair. Lazarus could only reflect on how grateful he was to have a friend who was willing to lay down his life for him.

JESUS THE CONSOLER

The risen Christ invites us to share our feelings of shame, guilt, grief, envy, fear, and anxiety with him in prayer and to allow him to console us. When praying over the accounts of Jesus' appearances to his mother and friends after his resurrection, Ignatius suggests that we "consider the office of consoler that Christ our Lord exercises, and compare it with the way in which friends are wont to console each other" (*Spiritual Exercises*, no. 224). It is important for us as post-Easter followers of Jesus to appreciate the ongoing role of the risen Jesus today as a consoler.

Spiritual consolation may not remove all our emotional pain, but it provides assurance and a quiet confidence that God is present in every aspect of our lives. In the Ignatian framework, spiritual consolation represents an inner sense of being connected to God in a caring relationship and thus can be experienced even in the midst of pain. For those who are sincerely trying to live loving lives, Ignatius states that God's presence can be detected through experiences of consolation, which manifests itself as any increase in faith, hope, love, a deeper capacity to trust, a sorrow for one's sins, and an increased desire for joyful and loving service. Ignatian consolation parallels the fruit of the Holy Spirit that St. Paul enumerates: love, joy, peace, patience, kindness, generosity, faithfulness, gentleness, and self-control (see Gal 5:22–23).

Spiritual consolation and desolation do not simply correspond to our range of pleasurable and painful emotions. Spiritual consolation is an affective movement that draws us toward God. Consolation does not always mean that we *feel* good; nor does desolation always mean that we feel bad. We can be feeling good emotionally and be in a state of spiritual desolation, according to Ignatius, if the good feelings lead us *away from God* or deaden our spiritual lives. For example, if we feel exuberant about financial success and security and, as a result, lose touch with our dependence on God, we are really in a state of desolation. On the other hand, we can feel emotionally low and, yet, be in a state of spiritual consolation if we feel strengthened in our faith and hope in

117

God. Someone grieving the death of a loved one, for instance, may experience an inexplicable yearning for greater intimacy with God and be comforted by God's presence empathizing and grieving with him or her. What differentiates spiritual consolation and spiritual desolation, according to Ignatius, is the direction toward which we are being inwardly led—either *toward God (consolation)* or *away from God (desolation)*. The consolation of the risen Jesus is the reassurance that, no matter how we are feeling at any given time, God is with us, holding us in love.

CHAPTER SIX

HEALING SHAME

"The 'no matter whatness' of God dissolves the toxicity of shame and fills us with tender mercy. Favorable, finally, and called by name...."[1]

—Gregory Boyle, SJ

To dissolve the toxicity of shame, we need to believe in our hearts, not just in our heads, that God's grace can work miracles in us. When we can take in and integrate the gospel message of God's unconditional love and acceptance, the painful effects of shame gradually dissolve as we come to know ourselves as God knows us: good, lovable, and precious. And, like Jesus at his baptism in the River Jordan, we discover our true identities and worth when we experience ourselves as God's beloved. As the waters of baptism streaked down his face, Jesus took in the message of divine love in a way that permeated his entire being. The heavens opened up and enabled him to hear the voice of God resounding in his heart: "You are my Son, the Beloved; with you I am well pleased" (Mark 1:11). In that moment, Jesus had a profound sense of being taken up, once and for all, into the embrace of God. Our own experience of "hearing" the voice of God addressing us in a personal and deeply affirming way need not be as dramatic as it was for Jesus. It may occur in ordinary ways—in the loving manner in which a friend calls out our name, or in the affectionate gaze of a loved one, or in the kind gesture of a stranger, or in a quiet voice within that reassures us that all will be well. These manifestations of God's love are just as real as Jesus' experience in the River Jordan. If we pay prayerful attention when going about our daily lives, we too can hear the voice of God as a sustaining and guiding presence. Biblical scholar Marcus Borg describes the myriad ways that God speaks to us:

> I think God "*speaks*" to us. I don't mean oral or aural revelation or divine dictation. But I think God "speaks" to us—sometimes dramatically in visions, less dramatically in some of our dreams, in internal "proddings" or "leadings," through people, and through the devotional practices and scriptures of our tradition. We sometimes have a sense—I sometimes have a sense—of being *addressed.*[2]

If, however, our images of God are largely negative—for example, if we imagine God as a disapproving parent, a strict judge, or a demanding boss—we will only hear what we expect to hear: we are unworthy of God's attention and love. The thought that God might really take delight in us will be drowned out by our own inner voices of shame.

ALLOWING OURSELVES TO BE LOVED

To receive God's love as an unearned gift may be a difficult concept to grasp. In addition to any negative images of God we might have, we are influenced, sometimes subtly, by cultural messages that find their way into our hearts and minds: messages to be self-reliant, independent, to be takers, not givers, and to secure our worth with money, power, and prestige. We thoughtlessly repeat slogans such as, "Every gift has its price," "There's no free lunch," "You've got to stand on your own two feet," and "God helps those who help themselves." The end result is that we mistrust the very notion that anyone, including God, would give to us out of pure love; we become suspicious of others' motives, afraid of being indebted to them if we accept a gift, or of appearing needy if we ask for help. To accept God's love as a free, unearned gift is to believe that God's love has no strings attached—that it comes without a hitch, without restrictions or fine print, and with no expiration date.

This is the kind of God that Jesus proclaimed when he preached that the love of God is universal and completely gratuitous.

In his *Spiritual Exercises*, Ignatius delineates the fundamental choice that confronts us as Christians (nos. 136–48). We either accept God's love as a free gift, or we try to earn it through our own efforts. These two opposing options—the first representing the way of Jesus; the second, the way of "the world"—vie for our allegiance. For Ignatius, the way of Jesus entails following the path of powerlessness and vulnerability, which leads to a humble reliance on God's love as the basis of our identities and worth. This is the path laid out in the first beatitude: "Blessed are the poor in spirit, for theirs is the kingdom of heaven" (Matt 5:3). When we acknowledge our powerlessness as human beings in the face of the many things that threaten our existence and well-being, we are admitting our poverty of spirit, our dependence on God. In the face of such uncontrollable realities as natural disasters, catastrophic illnesses, and random accidents, the way of Jesus encourages us to put our trust in God. This humble stance is reflected in the Fisherman's Prayer, associated with those who toil in the treacherous sea off Gloucester, Massachusetts: "Help us, O God, for thy sea is so great and my boat is so small." God's love will uphold and sustain us at every moment, not because we deserve it or have earned it, but because we are God's beloved. Acknowledging our dependence, we surrender our lives into the hands of God. Those who are familiar with Twelve-Step spirituality will recognize how closely the first three steps correspond with the way of Jesus, which encourages us to let God be God for us.

In contrast to the way of Jesus is the way of the world, an alternative path that lures us away from God. The way of the world encourages us to place our security in the accumulation of riches and honors. Material possessions, fame, and status become the basis on which we claim our right to be loved. This is ultimately a nonrelational path because it encourages us to be self-centered and self-sufficient, dependent on no one but ourselves—we "stand on our own two feet" and "make it on our own." It encourages us to value money over people and success over love and compassion. In contrast to the way of Jesus, which leads to humility, the way of the world leads to pride and alienation, deluding us into thinking that God's love is earned by our own efforts. It consigns us to lives of ongoing anxiety and obsession with earning and achieving. And in a subtle way, it promotes shame because when our ultimate goals are riches and success, we live in anticipation of being humiliated by failure.

THE HEALING OF SHAME

While many theories exist about the nature of shame, there is substantial agreement that shame is a social emotion that is concerned with how we are regarded by others. Rejection by others— real or imagined—is what causes shame. Not being accepted for who we are wounds us deeply and persuades us that we are worthless and unlovable. Acceptance and belonging are as essential for our emotional well-being as food and water are for our physical well-being. When others truly see and accept us for who we are, we feel valued and have a sense of well-being. In contrast, when we feel rejected by others—be they family, friends, neighbors, or colleagues—we feel a sense of dread, that something is wrong, and then we feel shame.

We are, and always will be, vulnerable to shame because we live in a culture that uses it to motivate and punish us. This means that in addition to the personal shame we each carry inside, we must contend with the shame that comes from without. According to studies on shame and dysfunctional systems, all of our institutions are shame-based, and we are constantly being appraised and judged according to other people's evaluations and standards. For example, educational institutions try to weed out "underperformers" for the sake of their reputations and competitive standing, and in the business world, personnel and business decisions are guided by productivity and profit—no matter the human cost.[3] The stresses of living in an evaluative and shaming society can be damaging to our sense of self unless we have close relationships that are not judging and shaming. The lives we have at home make a crit-ical difference to our emotional, physical, and spiritual well-being. If we are fortunate enough to have family, friends, or a community who love us for who we are—with our strengths and weaknesses, successes and failures—we are better equipped to deal with the harsh realities of the society in which we live.

Yet, no matter how loved we are by family and friends, we will still have our private dark nights, times when we feel lost, alone, not good enough. At times such as these, when even God seems absent, it is important to have spiritual practices and rituals that can sustain us and contain our fears and anxieties. While we can-not help but be influenced by the values of the world in which we live, we do not have to conform to or be controlled by those val-ues. The Christian path, as expressed in the Beatitudes and mod-eled by Christ, is clearly countercultural. But to follow it requires that we be grounded in our faith-identities and that we develop spiritual lives that nourish and sustain us, especially during times of darkness.

Christian faith can be a strong buffer in the face of rejection, whether that rejection comes from the outside world or from within ourselves. Faith, according to theologian Paul Tillich, is "the courage to accept our acceptability despite feelings of unac-ceptability."[4] "Feelings of unacceptability" accurately captures the experience of shame. Faith is the invitation to believe, in the midst of our "feelings of unacceptability," that God accepts us totally and unconditionally. The healing of shame through faith requires more than an intellectual assent to God's love; it takes a profound expe-rience of being "struck by grace." While we cannot make this hap-pen, we can, through prayer, open ourselves to be touched by such a transforming grace. Tillich vividly describes this experience:

> Do you know what it means to be struck by grace? We cannot transform our lives, unless we allow them to be transformed by the stroke of grace. It happens or it does not happen. And certainly it does not happen if we try to force it upon ourselves, just as it shall not happen so

long as we think, in our self-complacency, that we have no need of it. Grace strikes us when we are in great pain and restlessness. It strikes us when, year after year, the longed-for perfection of life does not appear, when the old compulsions reign within us as they have for decades, when despair destroys all joy and courage. Sometimes at that moment a shaft of light breaks into our darkness, and it is as though a voice were saying: "You are accepted. You are accepted," accepted by that which is greater than you, and the name of which you do not know. Do not ask for the name now, perhaps you will find it later. Do not try to do anything now; perhaps later you will do much. Do not seek for anything; do not perform anything; do not intend anything. Simply accept the fact that you are accepted. If that happens to us, we experience grace.[5]

SELF-ACCEPTANCE BASED ON GOD'S LOVE

In addition to reassuring us of God's acceptance, faith also encourages us to let go of lingering feelings of self-hatred and self-rejection that stem from past experiences of shame. As our earlier discussion of the sources of shame makes clear, the shame we feel is, for the most part, the result of experiences beyond our control. Acknowledging this enables us to replace self-blame with self-compassion. Compassion toward oneself entails being empathic and caring of one's "inner child." Psychologically, the notion of the "inner child" refers to emotional memories that are stored within and carry the lingering pain of unresolved childhood wounds. The inner child represents a vulnerable aspect of ourselves that we tend to abandon because we are ashamed of it. As adults, we need to recognize our neglected inner child and develop a healing relationship with it. A metaphor for our vulnerability, the inner child needs to be seen, soothed, and loved. We suggest a prayer exercise below, based on the Gospel story of children being brought to Jesus to be touched and blessed (see Mark 10:13–16), as a way of bringing this aspect of ourselves into the healing presence of God. Ultimately, our self-acceptance is an act of faith in a God who created us and deemed us to be good. If God loves and cares for us unconditionally, how can we justify withholding that same kind of love and acceptance from ourselves? It is the ultimate in pride to think that our standards for acceptability can be higher than God's. If we have suffered from deep feelings of shame all our lives, we must be converted from the belief that "I am not good enough" to the belief that "What I am is enough—enough for God's love and enough for my own joyful embrace."

ACKNOWLEDGING OUR SHAME

By the time we are adults, we have learned to live around our shame, successfully bypassing it with the help of the defense mechanisms described in chapter 1. So adept are we at not feeling shame, that we may have difficulty recognizing it in ourselves. For most people, shame commonly takes the form of an overall sense of low self-esteem.[6] It is the shame that comes from feeling unattractive, inadequate, weak, shy, flawed, stupid, rejected, intimidated, or ineffectual. It is the shame we have felt as long as we can remember. A client's journal entry shows the staying power of everyday shame, and how we don't "just get over it" or outgrow it, but rather continue to suffer it long after the circumstances that caused it are gone:

> I am stuck here with a poor image of self that has a louder voice than I can bear at times. While I have all the support around me, the scars from high school remain. I have sought help and received it. The ups and downs continue. Being drawn to look lumpy and fat on a white board by three insecure and mean boys when I was a junior in high school, remains with me. I look at my clothes, the waist size of my pants before I get into them, amazed

every time that they fit and are not too small. What I see in the mirror has been deeply scarred by what happened over ten years ago. While I diet now and then with results, recognize my physical strength, and eat healthy, I am never enough. My progress is never enough....When I thought of myself before this day when I was bullied in high school, I was okay, never really considering the possibility that I may ever appear fat or lumpy. Now, I am afraid of being that image on the white board.

Many of us can recall similar stories when a person or situation left us feeling ashamed and defenseless. A shaming experience may scar our self-image and continue to dog us, even when we know intellectually that it happened years ago. We may try to move past it and forget about it, and to some extent we succeed, but when the memory comes back to us, we feel the shame all over again.

In the remainder of this chapter, we present what we believe to be an initial step in healing the effects of shame: recalling shameful experiences and feelings so that we can bring them into our prayer, the place where God meets us in our pain. The suffering that we have kept out of our prayer, and out of God's reach, we now choose to bring to God, who desires to heal us and make us whole. Transforming the effects of shame is not a solitary process. In therapy and in spiritual direction, it is the experience of being heard, seen, and emotionally held that is healing. Likewise, if prayer is to be healing and transforming, we must be willing to let God into our hurt by acknowledging our shameful feelings. We cannot heal ourselves by ourselves; we need another to bear witness to our pain, to truly see us, and to embrace and console us. The following way of proceeding may be helpful:

1. It is important to begin to recognize shame in your life. Notice the ways that you shame yourself. "That was stupid." "You look terrible today." "You'll never be as smart as..." "Who cares what you have to say?" "They don't really like you." Now, notice how others

are shaming you. "Let me show you the right way." "I can't believe you could be so dumb." "Didn't you ever learn how to do that?" "You ate all that?" "Don't you know that coat is out of date?"

2. Understand the origins of your shame. When did it begin? How did it start? Recall one of your most shaming experiences as a child. What do you remember? Pay attention to how you felt. How did you deal with it at the time?

3. How do you experience and deal with shame now? How do you conceal it? What defenses do you use to avoid feeling shame?

4. How do you think shame has affected your relationship with others? With God?

5. Now, imagine yourself in a situation that caused you great shame. What do you wish someone had done to help you feel better? What words would have comforted you?

6. Imagine Jesus saying those words to you now. Look at Jesus as you listen to his words. Can you take in the compassion in his eyes? Let his words touch your heart. Pay attention to how you feel.

7. Practice self-empathy. Imagine treating yourself with the same respect and compassion that you feel from Jesus.

8. Practice self-forgiveness. Forgive yourself for the self-blame and self-hatred you thought you deserved.

To enter into this kind of intimate prayer in which you allow yourself to be transparent before God, you must trust God enough to expose your vulnerability and pain. The shameful, fearful parts of you that hide in secrecy need to be reassured that God will embrace and hold them. The Jesuit poet Gerard Manly Hopkins encourages this kind of prayer when he suggests that we hand over our pains and struggles to God's keeping, trusting that God will care for us even more than we care for ourselves:

...deliver it, early now, long before death
Give beauty back, beauty, beauty, beauty, back to God,
    beauty's self and beauty's giver.
See; not a hair is, not an eyelash, not the least lash lost;
    every hair
Is, hair of the head, numbered.

In the next stanza, he acknowledges how vulnerable we are to being overwhelmed by anxiety and insecurity and then reassures us that everything in our lives—whether big or small—is held onto, understood, and cared for by a loving God:

O then, weary then why should we tread? O why are we so
    haggard at
    the heart, so care-coiled, care-killed, so fagged, so fashed,
      so cogged,
    so cumbered,
When the thing we freely forfeit is kept with fonder a care,
Fonder a care than we could have kept it,...[7]

IMAGINATIVE CONTEMPLATION AND THE HEALING OF SHAME

Imaginative contemplation of Gospel stories is a powerful spiritual tool for the healing and transformation of shame. It disposes us to hear the word of God being addressed to us personally, in the present, opening our hearts to take in the good news that we are God's beloved. Trusting that God loves us unconditionally—defects and all—we bring the shame-filled parts of ourselves into prayer so that they can be touched by grace.

It was Ignatius's hope that using this method of prayer would bring us "felt-knowledge" (*sentir*) of God's love for us, not merely "head-knowledge." This personal knowledge goes beyond grasping something conceptually or intellectually. It involves realizing something emotionally, in a way that affects our whole being.

Felt-knowledge is something we know from direct, immediate experience, not from reading or hearsay. In other words, what we desire in contemplating scripture is an experience by which we know "in our bones" that God loves us with unconditional and unwavering love. The following prayer exercises are designed to help heal the shame that prevents us from having a close personal relationship with God. These suggestions are intended only to be an illustration or template of how an imaginative prayer can unfold. Strictly speaking, the Ignatian method encourages a more spontaneous and unscripted insertion of oneself into the biblical story than these guided prayers might suggest.

In practicing imaginative contemplation, it is important not to run ahead of grace. In other words, you should proceed only as you feel drawn, without exerting any force or pressure to make things happen. If you find yourself unable to move beyond a certain point, you should stay there for the time being and reflect on what can be learned in this experience. If, for instance, you feel strongly put off by something in a passage or feel a strong reluctance to participate in a gospel event, reflecting on these feelings can provide some insight into your current spiritual and psychological state. Imaginative contemplation is most fruitful when you spontaneously allow grace to guide you, in a personally unique way, into the healing presence of God through whatever scriptural passage you are using.

Being the Beloved of God

Biblical Passage

The Baptism of Jesus in the Jordan (see Mark 1:9–11; Matt 3:13–17; Luke 3:21–22)

Prayer Experience

1. Find a quiet place where you can be alone and undisturbed for a period of thirty to forty-five minutes.
2. Say a brief prayer acknowledging the presence of God as you enter into prayer and ask for the grace to be open to the healing touch of God.

3. Read the text a couple of times slowly and take in the event that the text is relating. What is happening and how does the action unfold? Who are the people involved? How do they feel about each other and what is occurring?

4. Put the text away. Now with the eyes of your imagination, see the dramatic action of the story unfold, as if you were witnessing the event as an outside observer.

5. Notice especially what Jesus experiences as his cousin, John the Baptist, pours water on his forehead. Imagine Jesus looking up and seeing the heavens part and then hearing the voice of the Creator of the universe say to him: "You are my Son, the Beloved; with you I am well pleased." As Jesus takes in what is happening to him, imagine his whole body being filled with the warm glow and fullness of God's affirming love.

6. Put yourself at the edge of the riverbank and imagine yourself somehow being drawn to John the Baptist to be baptized and to enjoy the same experience that Jesus had.

7. Imagine yourself tentatively dipping your feet into the river and feeling the soft mud at the river's bottom ooze gently through your toes. Then you start to move toward the middle more boldly because you find the water warm and welcoming.

8. See yourself standing in line, waiting your turn. Suddenly you find yourself in front of the Baptist, and he starts to pour water on your forehead. At that moment, you look up and see the heavens part and you hear the voice of the Creator of the universe say to you: "You are my Beloved; with you I am well pleased."

9. When you hear these words, you feel your whole body warm up with the flow of God's affirming love. Remain in that moment and absorb what has just been addressed to you. Allow God's reassuring voice

to resonate deeply throughout your being, filling your inner pockets of emptiness and shame with healing love.

Comments on the Exercise

Because early experiences of shame leave us with a deeply rooted conviction that we are defective in some fundamental way and therefore unworthy of love, the experience of seeing ourselves as God's beloved is like being "struck by grace." Our sense of ourselves is transformed, and we can begin to take delight in ourselves because we know that God delights in us. For some, the grace that is sought in this contemplation can be felt at the actual time of prayer, and they feel deeply consoled by God's love. Sometimes, however, people receive the grace of knowing deeply that they are the beloved in an experience outside of prayer. They experience something in life that profoundly affirms their goodness. Because experience is the language of God, as Ignatian spirituality holds, we can hear God expressing delight in us through these "Jordan River experiences in life." Notice that Jesus' affirming experience in the Jordan River took place *before* the start of his public ministry. This fact highlights the truth that God's love for us, as it was for Jesus, is based on our being, not on our doing. God loved us into being and continues to sustain us, not through any merit of our own, but because we are who we are.

An Experience of Being Positively Mirrored

Biblical Passage

The Presentation of Jesus in the Temple (see Luke 2:22–38)

Prayer Experience

1. Begin by following the first four steps of the previous prayer exercise, "Being the Beloved of God."
2. With the eyes of your imagination, see Joseph and Mary with the infant Jesus in Mary's arms climbing

the steep steps of the temple in Jerusalem. As they
enter the section of the temple where the child is to
be presented to God, a holy man named Simeon
approaches them. Moving aside the cloth covering
the baby's face, he bends close to get a good look at
the child. Notice how he beams with joy and excite-
ment as he looks long and lovingly into the infant's
eyes. He then straightens up and, with a heart burst-
ing with gratitude and praise, he prays:

Master, now you are dismissing your servant in peace,
    according to your word;
for my eyes have seen your salvation,
    which you have prepared in the presence of all peoples,
a light for revelation to the Gentiles
    and for glory to your people Israel.

(Luke 2:29–32)

3. Just as Simeon finishes praying, Anna, the eighty-
four year old prophetess who spends her days in the
temple serving God with fasting and prayer, comes
by. She too looks long and lovingly at the child Jesus
and breaks out in praise because she sees in the face
of this baby the promised Messiah, sent by God to
establish the kingdom of God.

4. Notice how the infant Jesus is so alert and attentive
to both Simeon and Anna as they hover over him
with admiration and love. Their warm smiles, gentle
touch, and adoring eyes fill Jesus with a deep sense of
being special and loved.

5. Now imagine that you are the infant in Mary's arms.
Joseph is there, as are Simeon and Anna. They draw
gently near to you and, by turn, ask to hold you. As
you are passed from one person to the next, you see
your own lovableness and specialness reflected in the
eyes of these adults who bend over you with such

obvious affection and appreciation. Imagine how their affirming reactions fill your being with a deep sense of your goodness.

Comments on the Exercise

Early experiences of shame leave us with feelings of unworthiness and of not being good enough to be loved. In infancy, we need to see our goodness mirrored in our parents' eyes as they gaze on us. Our need to feel cherished and loved—to be the center of someone's world—is a basic need of every child. When our narcissistic needs are not adequately met, for whatever reason, our sense of self is wounded and we are left feeling fundamentally unlovable and unattractive to others and to God. Imaginative prayer can be healing in that it invites us to bring our wounded child to the temple in Jerusalem, as Mary and Joseph did with Jesus, so that we can experience being loved and cherished as the infant Jesus did.

Our Past Hurts and the Love of God

Biblical Passage

Jesus and the Children (see Mark 10:13–16)

Prayer Experience

1. Again, begin by following the first four steps of the prayer exercise on page 129, "Being the Beloved of God."
2. With the eyes of the imagination, see how parents are rushing to Jesus, bringing their little children for him to touch. Seeing this, the disciples react quickly to stop them because they are concerned that Jesus needs some time alone to rest. But Jesus scolds the disciples for trying to prevent the children from coming close to him.
3. Notice how Jesus reaches out and hugs each of the children. Then he lays his hands on them and blesses them.

Experience how secure and loved each child feels as he or she is being embraced and blessed by Jesus.

4. Imagine that you are taking your inner child to Jesus so that you too can be touched. Just as you arrive, Jesus is blessing the last of the children gathered about him and the disciples. You walk up and stand in front of him. Jesus smiles warmly at you and invites you to sit next to him. You hesitate and slowly move closer. Putting his arm around your shoulders, he encourages you to tell him how you have been hurt. As the compassionate and understanding face of Jesus acknowledges the hurts you have experienced, you feel deeply reassured of your own lovableness.

Comments on the Exercise

Excessive shame is often the result of not having been embraced in a way that reassures us of our goodness and lovableness. Warm and caring touch is important for the healthy development of infants. Many hospitals have started "volunteer cuddler programs" because "studies in the neonatal intensive care units indicate that infants who are regularly held, stroked, and spoken to gain weight faster and leave the hospital sooner than those who are not."[8] If there is a place in us that feels that it was not "regularly held, stroked, and spoken to," praying over the passage of Jesus and the children using imaginative contemplation can be a way of opening this hurt within us to God's healing grace.

Fear of Abandonment and the Love of God

Biblical Passage

Jesus and the Children (see Mark 10:13–16)

Prayer Experience

If we felt abandoned in childhood, either physically or emotionally, we live in fear that it will happen again. Children feel abandoned when they are physically separated from a parent because of death, divorce, or displacement due to war or economic necessity. They may feel abandoned if their parents are so consumed with their own struggles with addiction, unemployment, or illness that they have little time and energy left to give to their needy children. Children tend to blame themselves for not getting the attention or affection they long for. When they are neglected, they feel shame, because they presume it is their fault. For anyone who identifies with this experience, it would be helpful to continue the prayer exercise of Jesus and the children in the following way:

1. Recall how old you were and how you looked when you felt hurt and alone as a child. Looking at an old photo would be helpful. Imagine yourself as that child sitting on Jesus' lap. Sense how Jesus intuits your discomfort with intimacy and your fear of being rejected and abandoned.
2. Wanting to comfort and reassure you, Jesus tells you of God's love for you. Like a parent soothing a fearful child by reading a story, Jesus recites the following verses from the Prophet Isaiah:

But Zion said, "The LORD has forsaken me,
    my Lord has forgotten me."
Can a woman forget her nursing child,
    or show no compassion for the child of her womb?
Even these may forget,
    yet I will not forget you.
See, I have inscribed you on the palms of my hands;
    your walls are continually before me.
(Isa 49:14–16)

3. Imagine that your shame and fear of abandonment dissipate as you listen to Jesus' gentle reminder of God's faithful love for you.

Called by Name

Biblical Passage

The Appearance to Mary of Magdala (see John 20:11–18)

Prayer Experience

1. Begin by following the first four steps of the prayer exercise on page 129, "Being the Beloved of God."
2. Imagine Mary outside of the tomb of Jesus, weeping. She peers inside the open tomb and finds Jesus' body missing. Two angels in white sitting where the body of Jesus had been ask her, "Woman, why are you weeping?" "They have taken my Lord away," she replies, "and I don't know where they have put him." Turning suddenly, she sees Jesus standing there, though she does not recognize him. Jesus says, "Woman, why are you weeping? Who are you looking for?" Mistaking him for the gardener, Mary answers, "Sir, if you have taken him away, tell me where you have put him, and I will go and remove him." Jesus says, "Mary!" At that moment, hearing Jesus say her name, she recognizes Jesus and reaches out to him.
3. You may want to reflect on this passage in the light of what Jesus said ten chapters before, when describing himself as the good shepherd:

   I am the good shepherd. I know my own and my own know me. (John 10:14)

   My sheep hear my voice. I know them, and they follow me. (John 10:27)
4. Imagine that you are roaming about the garden of your ordinary life, feeling ashamed, lonely, and empty. Suddenly you bump into a stranger who, to your surprise, calls you by your name. The very moment you hear the loving and endearing way your name is called out, you feel deeply loved and accepted.

Comments on the Exercise

In this prayer exercise, we ask for the grace to recognize the voice of the risen Jesus calling out our names with affection and warmth, just as he spoke Mary's name in the garden. For some, the affirming voice is heard in the solitude of prayer; for others, it is through the way a loved one calls their name. In either case, it is an experience that can bring healing to the parts of us that suffer from not being seen, recognized, and valued for our unique selves.

REMINDED OF OUR LOVELINESS

For most of us, self-esteem is something we hold tenuously. Moments of shame make us forget who we really are: God's beloved whose worth derives from this. Imaginative prayer can help us to stay centered in our true identities, and it also can help us recall who we are in God's eyes when we get stuck in our shame-based identities. We depend on God and those who love us to remind us, because we easily forget, that we are lovable and loved. Poet Galway Kinnell beautifully expresses the affirming nature of love in the following poem:

> The bud
> stands for all things
> even for those things that don't flower,
> for everything flowers, from within, of self-blessing;
> though sometimes it is necessary
> to reteach a thing its loveliness...
> and to retell it in words and in touch
> it is lovely.[9]

To live with self-compassion and self-love can be an ongoing struggle. Christian faith challenges us to imitate God's unconditional love by lovingly accepting ourselves without condition. The ability to peacefully embrace all aspects of ourselves, even the less lovely aspects, brings a sense of wholeness where there was once self-alienation. As our self-acceptance deepens, our shame is transformed into humility, and we realize that we are limited, yet good enough to be loved.

Throughout the seasons of our lives, the God who causes the sun to shine on the good and the bad and lets the rain fall on the just and the unjust never fails to bathe our existence with abundant grace and acceptance. The heavenly voice that addressed Jesus in the Jordan as the beloved seeks to convey the same divine affirmation to each of us today: "*You* are my Beloved; with you I am well pleased." Only when we allow this divine affirmation to permeate our hearts and to reverberate throughout our being will we experience our loveliness, rooted in God's unconditional love. God's love not only makes us come to be, but also makes us good *in our very being*. God's love for us is foundational because it both establishes us in life and causes us to be lovable. As the book of Wisdom states:

> Yes, you love everything that exists, and nothing that you have made disgusts you, since, if you had hated something, you would not have made it. And how could a thing subsist, had you not willed it? Or how be preserved, if not called forth by you? No, you spare all, since all is yours, Lord, lover of life! For your imperishable spirit is in everything. (Wis 11:24–27 NJB)

Humble acceptance of ourselves comes to us when we realize in our hearts that we are loved by God gratuitously and not for any of our personal attributes or qualities, talents or accomplishments. When this happens, shame no longer has the power to overwhelm us and rob us of our joy and peace.

NOTES

Introduction

1. Annie Murphy Paul, "Your Brain on Fiction," *New York Times*, as cited in Gabrielle Cohen, "Imaginary Beings," *Spirituality and Health* (March/April 2013): 68.

2. Ibid.

3. T. M. Luhrmann, *When God Talks Back: Understanding the American Evangelical Relationship with God* (New York: Vintage Books, 2012), 104.

4. Ibid., 105.

5. Ibid.

6. Elaine M. Prevallet, "Living in the Mercy," *Weaving: A Journal of the Christian Spiritual Life* 15, no. 5 (September/October 2000): 7.

CHAPTER ONE:
The Challenge to Loving

1. James M. Bowler, "Shame: A Primary Root of Resistance to Movement in Direction," *Presence: The Journal of Spiritual Directors International* 3, no. 3 (September 1997): 27.

2. Vern Rutsala in "Shame" by James M. Schutz, *Reflections on Psychology, Culture, and Life: The Jung Page*, August 21, 2006, http://www.cgjungpage.org/learn/articles/analytical-psychology/776-shame.

3. Speaking on Vatican Radio on April 29, 2013. See also Cindy Wooden, "Pope, with Fellow Jesuits, Prays for 'Grace of Shame,' Humility," *Catholic News Service*, USCCB, July 31, 2013.

4. Eric Clapton, *Clapton: The Autobiography* (New York: Broadway Books, 2007), 235–36.

5. Ibid.

6. Roberta C. Bondi, *In Ordinary Times: Healing the Wounds of the Heart* (Nashville, TN: Abingdon Press, 1996), 86.

7. Joe McHugh, *Startled by God: Wisdom from Unexpected Places* (Cincinnati, Ohio: Franciscan Media, 2013), 25.

8. Robert C. Morris, "God's Wrestling Match with Wrath," *Weavings: A Journal of the Christian Life* 15, no. 5 (September/October 2000): 21.

9. Helen Cepero, *Christ-Shaped Character: Choosing Love, Faith, and Hope* (Downer Grove, Illinois: IVP Books, 2014), 50.

10. Ibid., 52.

11. U.S. Department of Health and Human Services, "The Child Abuse Prevention and Treatment Act" (2010), 6.

12. Rosemary S. L. Mills, "Taking Stock of the Developmental Literature on Shame," *Developmental Review* 25 (2005): 37.

13. Anne Lamott, *Grace (Eventually): Thoughts on Faith* (New York: Riverhead Books, 2007), 42–43.

14. Ibid., 77–78.

15. Johannes B. Metz, *Poverty of Spirit*, trans. John Drury (Mahwah, NJ: Paulist Press, 1968), 7–8.

16. Ibid.

17. Karen Horney, *Neurosis and Human Growth* (New York: W. W. Norton & Company, 1950), 64–65.

CHAPTER TWO:

Imaging God, Imaging Self

1. Wm. Paul Young, "All Things Considered," *National Public Radio*, December 1, 2012.

2. Antony F. Campbell, *God First Loved Us: The Challenge of Accepting Unconditional Love* (Mahwah, NJ: Paulist Press, 2000), 80.

3. Ibid.

4. Ibid., 77.

5. Ibid., 82.

6. Bonnie Ware, *The Top Five Regrets of the Dying: A Life Transformed by the Dearly Departing* (Carlsbad, CA: Hay House, Inc., 2011).

7. Campbell traces out these consequences throughout *God First Loved Us*.

8. Michael Himes, "Living Conversation: Higher Education in a Catholic Context," in *An Ignatian Spirituality Reader*, ed. George W. Traub (Chicago: Loyola Press, 2008), 228.

9. Campbell, *God First Loved Us*, 10.

10. Gregory Baum, *Man Becoming: God in Secular Experience* (New York: Herder and Herder, 1971), 194–95.

11. Helen Schungel-Straumann, "Gott als Mutter in Hosea 11," *Theologische Quartalschrift* 166, no. 2 (1986): 119–34, in *Theological Digest* 34, no. 1 (Spring 1987): 7.

12. Ibid., 6.

13. Ibid., 8.

14. Ibid., 7.

15. Ibid., 179.

16. Ann Belford Ulanov, *Picturing God* (Boston: Cowley Publications, 1986), 164.

17. Ana-Maria Rizzuto, *The Birth of the Living God: A Psychoanalytic Study* (Chicago: The University of Chicago Press, 1979), 200.

18. Ibid., 47.

19. John Westerhoff, *Spiritual Life: The Foundation for Preaching and Teaching* (Louisville, KY: Westminster John Knox Press, 1994), 4.

20. Arthur W. Combs, "The Perceptual Approach to Good Teaching," in *Humanistic Education Source Handbook*, ed. Donald A. Reed and Sidney B. Simon (Englewood Cliffs, NJ: Prentice Hall, Inc., 1975), 254.

21. William Meissner, "The Psychology of Religious Experience," *Communio* 4 (1977): 53.

22. Rizzuto distinguishes between the concept of God and one's God representation. The concept of God roughly parallels what we are referring to as one's professed image of God, and one's

God representation parallels what we term one's operative image of God. "When dealing with the concrete fact of belief, it is important to clarify the conceptual and emotional differences between the concept of God and the images of God which, combined in multiple forms, produce the prevailing God representation in a given individual at a given time. The concept of God is fabricated mostly at the level of secondary-process thinking. This is the God of the theologians, the God whose existence or nonexistence is debated by metaphysical reasoning. But this God leaves us cold....Even someone who believes intellectually that there *must* be a God may feel no inclination to accept him unless images of previous interpersonal experience have fleshed out the concept with multiple images that can now coalesce in a representation that he can accept emotionally. This God provides and evokes a multitude of feelings, images, and memories connected with the earlier childhood elaboration of the representation of God and to that representation's later elaborations" (Rizzuto, *Birth of the Living God*, 47–48).

23. Gerard W. Hughes, *God of Surprises* (Mahwah, NJ: Paulist Press, 1985), 36–37.

24. J. B. Phillips, *Your God Is Too Small* (New York: The Macmillan Company, 1961), 54.

25. Donald McCullough, *The Trivialization of God* (Colorado Springs, CO: Navpress Publishing Group, 1995).

26. Thomas Merton, *Raids on the Unspeakable* (New York: New Directions, 1964), 85–86.

27. T. M. Luhrmann, *When God Talks Back: Understanding the American Evangelical Relationship with God* (New York: Random House, 2012), 330–31.

28. Ibid., 124.

29. Rizzuto, *Birth of the Living God*, 200.

30. Ibid., 46.

31. Campbell, *God First Loved Us*, 86.

32. Ibid., 33.

CHAPTER THREE:
Seeing with the Heart

1. Anne Lamott, *Help, Thanks, Wow: The Three Essential Prayers* (New York: Riverhead Books, 2012), 21.

2. Howard Gray, "Imagination," in *The New Westminster Dictionary of Christian Spirituality*, ed. Philip Sheldrake (Louisville, KY: Westminster John Knox Press, 2005), 361.

3. George Bernard Shaw, *St. Joan: A Chronicle Play in Six Scenes and an Epilogue* (New York: Viking Penguin Inc., 1924), 58–59.

4. Ann and Barry Ulanov, *The Healing Imagination: The Meeting of Psyche and Soul* (Einsiedeln, Switzerland: Daimon Verlag, 1999), 3.

5. Richard M. Gula, "Using Scripture in Prayer and Spiritual Direction," *Spirituality Today* 36, no. 4 (Winter 1984): 301.

6. T. M. Luhrmann, *When God Talks Back: Understanding the American Evangelical Relationship with God* (New York: Random House, 2012), xxii.

7. Gray, "Imagination," 361.

8. Nickel Creek, vocal performance of "The Hand Song," by Sean Watkins and David Puckett, recorded in 1999 on *Nickel Creek* (Sugar Hill Records, 2000).

9. Elizabeth A. Johnson, "The Incomprehensibility of God and the Image of God Male and Female," in *Women's Spirituality: Resources for Christian Development*, ed. Joann Wolski Conn (Mahwah, NJ: Paulist Press, 1986), 243.

10. Luhrmann, *When God Talks Back*, 178.

11. William C. Spohn, "The Biblical Theology of the Pastoral Letter and Ignatian Contemplation," *Studies in the Spirituality of Jesuits* 17, no. 4 (1985): 8–9.

12. Ibid., 10.

13. C. G. Jung, as quoted in Anthony Stevens, *Jung* (New York: Oxford University Press, 1994), 109.

14. Jesuit psychologist Brendan Callaghan provides a helpful explanation of how depth psychology might understand what takes place in Ignatian imaginative prayer with scripture. The *Spiritual Exercises* of Ignatius, proven to be a powerful transformative process over the centuries, feature praying with the imagination prominently. In fact, 135 of the 150 prayer periods of a month-long experience of the Exercises entail the use of the imagination. In these periods of imaginative prayer, we encounter the central symbols and images of scripture that make up our Christian faith and order our lives. Creation and the gift of life from God, forgiveness and the merciful love of God, and vocation and the call to collaborate with God's project on earth are examples of such biblical symbols. These symbols function like psychological archetypes that emerge from our unconscious, suggesting psychic or human potentials for more expansive living. "In the Exercises Ignatius puts me regularly in contact with the key symbols of my living: should we be surprised if I am transformed by this repeated experience?" poses Callaghan. "But the symbols are symbols: should we therefore be surprised if they too are transformed in this dialogue?" In other words, imaginative engagement with the symbols of faith contained in scripture "permits these symbols—inevitably shaped individually by my unconscious—to be reshaped in ways that reflect my growth and development." Brendan Callaghan, "Do Teddy Bears Make Good Spiritual Directors? Ignatius Loyola Meets Donald Winnicott," *The Way* 42, no. 3 (July 2003): 29.

15. Winnicott referred to this function of the imagination as engaging in a healthy way with illusion. Unlike Freud's negative understanding of illusion as an immature flight from the real world, Winnicott, among others, saw a more positive role of illusion in human life. For him, it was a source of truth, capable of revealing life-giving alternatives for living and relating, because the "creative intuition fostered in the transitional space is a crucial human form of knowing." James W. Jones, "Playing and Believing: D. W. Winnicott," in *Religion, Society and Psychoanalysis*, ed. Janet L. Jacobs and Donald Capps (Boulder: Westview Press, 1997),

117–18, as quoted in Callaghan, "Do Teddy Bears Make Good Spiritual Directors?" 24.

16. Patrick Purnell, *Imagine* (Oxford: Way Books, 2003), viii.

CHAPTER FOUR:

Jesus as the Compassion of God

1. Marcus Borg, *The Heart of Christianity: Rediscovering a Life of Faith* (New York: HarperCollins, 2004), 88.
2. Shusaku Endo, *A Life of Jesus*, trans. Richard A. Schuchert (Mahwah, New Jersey: Paulist Press, 1973), 57.
3. *National Catholic Reporter*, quoted on the back cover of Endo, *A Life of Jesus*.
4. Endo, *A Life of Jesus*, 1.
5. Edmund Colledge and James Walsh, trans. *Julian of Norwich: Showings* (Mahwah, NJ: Paulist Press, 1978), chap. 57.
6. Ibid., chap. 61.
7. Ibid., chap. 54.
8. Ibid., chap. 5.
9. Monika K. Hellwig, *Jesus: The Compassion of God* (Wilmington, DE: Michael Glazier, Inc., 1983), 82–83.
10. Gregory Boyle, *Tattoos on the Heart: The Power of Boundless Compassion* (New York: Free Press, 2010), 52.
11. Anne Lamott, *Grace (Eventually): Thoughts on Faith* (New York: Riverhead Books, 2007), 129.
12. Marion Woodman, *Addiction to Perfection: The Still Unravished Bride* (Toronto: Inner City Books, 1982), 10.
13. Endo, *A Life of Jesus*, 73.
14. Ibid., 60.
15. Stephen Mitchell, *The Gospel According to Jesus* (New York: HarperPerennial, 1991), 36.
16. Ignatius of Loyola, *The Spiritual Exercises of St. Ignatius*, trans. Louis J. Puhl (Chicago: Loyola University Press, 1951), nos. 102 and 106.
17. Ibid., no. 224.
18. Boyle, *Tattoos on the Heart*, 62.

145

19. Helen Prejean, *Dead Man Walking* (New York: Vintage Books, 1994). See also John Bookser Feister, "Sister Helen Prejean: The Real Woman Behind *Dead Man Walking*," *St. Anthony Messenger* (April 1996), http://americancatholic.org/messenger/Apr1996/feature1.asp.

20. Arthur Jones, "Bishop's Life Story as a Quest for Grace," *National Catholic Reporter*, July 12, 1996.

21. Gerard Manley Hopkins, "As Kingfishers Catch Fire," in *Hearts on Fire: Praying with Jesuits*, ed. Michael Harter (St. Louis: Institute of Jesuit Sources, 1993), 59.

CHAPTER FIVE: Gospel Stories of Consoling Love

1. Joe McHuge, *Startled by God: Wisdom from Unexpected Places* (Cincinnati, Ohio: Franciscan Media, 2013), xvii.

2. Richard M. Gula, "Using Scripture in Prayer and Spiritual Direction," *Spirituality Today* 36, no. 4 (Winter 1984): 301.

3. Ibid., 303.

4. Anthony de Mello, "The Look of Jesus," in *The Song of the Bird* (Garden City, NY: Image Books, 1984), 113–14.

CHAPTER SIX:
Healing Shame

1. Gregory Boyle, *Tattoos on the Heart: The Power of Boundless Compassion* (New York: Free Press, 2010), 60.

2. Marcus Borg, *The Heart of Christianity: Rediscovering a Life of Faith* (New York: HarperCollins, 2004), 73.

3. A 2014 FBI report cites that the number of sudden mass shootings in the United States has nearly tripled in recent years, and "Seventy percent of the shooters attacked schools or workplaces." ("Mass Shootings in the U.S. Have Seen Steep Rise," *Los Angeles Times*, September 25, 2014, AA2.)

4. Paul Tillich, *The Courage To Be* (New Haven: Yale University Press, 1952), 164–65; 172–73.

5. Paul Tillich, "You Are Accepted," chap. 19 in *The Shaking of the Foundations* (New York: Charles Scribner's Sons, 1948).

6. Sadly, some people suffer from the kind of acute shame that is so devastating that it leads to suicide or violence. Shame is toxic when the future seems hopeless and people are desperate to put an end to their pain and humiliation. There is an increasingly high incidence of suicide and violent acting out among young people today. Some of these instances involve gay and lesbian teenagers who have been "outed" in school or humiliated by cyber-bullying. They reach a breaking point. We are no longer shocked by news reports of school shootings, even massacres, by students who were retaliating because they felt ostracized and ridiculed for being "different." Even young children can be victims or perpetra-tors of violence in the form of bullying. These shame-related prob-lems clearly require the immediate care and attention of professionals. That is why school administrators and public health officials conduct workshops for teachers and parents on how to rec-ognize and deal with bullying. While the underlying causes of these problems should not be oversimplified, one social commentator believes the American culture of shame is partly to blame: "Our children grow up watching reality shows where boorish behavior is rewarded and insults, taunts and racist remarks hike ratings and create stars. And nothing is off-limits for criticism on countless makeover programs. Your clothes, your voice, your cooking, your weight...judges find fault with everything, while contestants try not to cry." (Sandy Banks, "Internet Intensifies Bullying," *Los Angeles Times*, Tuesday, October 22, 2013, A2).

7. Gerard Manley Hopkins, "The Leaden Echo and the Golden Echo," in *Poems and Prose of Gerard Manley Hopkins*, ed. W. H. Gardner (Baltimore, MD: Penguin Books, Inc., 1953), 53–54.

8. *Today's Headlines* (newsletter of Daniel Freeman Hospitals, Los Angeles, CA), April 6, 1994.

9. Galway Kinnell, "Saint Francis and the Sow," in *Three Books* (Boston: Houghton Mifflin, 2002), 81.